Natural Symbols

MARY DOUGLAS

Natural Symbols

Explorations in Cosmology

VINTAGE BOOKS
A DIVISION OF RANDOM HOUSE
NEW YORK

FIRST VINTAGE BOOKS EDITION, October 1973

Copyright © 1970, 1973 by Mary Douglas

All rights reserved under International and Pan-American
Copyright Conventions. Published in the United States
by Random House, Inc., New York. Originally published
in Great Britain by Barrie & Rockliff in 1970, and by
Pelican Books in 1973. Published in the United States
by Pantheon Books, a division of Random House, Inc.
in 1970.

Library of Congress Cataloging in Publication Data

Douglas, Mary (Tew)
  Natural symbols.
  Bibliography: p.
  1. Religion.   2. Ritual.   3. Symbolism.
I. Title.
[BL48.D67 1973]   113   73–5908
ISBN 0–394–71942–5

Manufactured in the United States of America

Contents

Diagrams

Acknowledgements

This book is obviously not intended solely for anthropologists. I hope it will be a bridge between anthropology and other disciplines. Yet anthropologists must be its most important critics, for only they can judge the soundness of my interpretations of field reports and bring up material which can either confirm or spoil my hypotheses. I have tried to limit myself to sources which are both accessible and of very high quality, so that if my uses of them seem idiosyncratic, anyone can go back to the original reports and check. But in the long run, as the perspectives I wish to develop have not been in the minds of field researchers, only new research, especially devised, can test these arguments.

It remains for me to thank those who have helped me most directly. First I thank the Dominicans at Blackfriars, Oxford, for inviting me to give the St Thomas Day lecture on 7 March 1968, and for publishing 'The Contempt of Ritual' in *New Blackfriars* (June, July 1968, 49: 475-82, 528-35), Theirs was the initial stimulus for the book. Further I thank Professor Kenneth Little and the Court of Edinburgh University for inviting me to deliver the Munro lectures in May 1968. For earlier work on this subject I am grateful to the Woldingham Association Committee and especially to Reverend Mother Eyre, Mary Don and Mona Macmillan. The research we hoped to promote on religious education has not yet been accomplished. At least this is offered as a sketch of some of the issues we hoped to tackle.

The first formal acknowledgement I must make is to Basil Bernstein. My debt to him is very apparent and I ask his pardon if the use I have made of his ideas is inept. I am grateful to the

Reverend Cornelius Ernst, OP, and to Peter Brown for reading the manuscript, and to David Schneider, Victor Turner and Nur Yalman for their discussions of lectures given on its basis in Chicago this year. I am also grateful to Bryan Wilson and Godfrey Lienhardt for kindly reading and commenting on parts of the manuscript, and to James Woodburn and to Daniel de Coppet for permission to quote from studies still awaiting publication and to Rodney Needham for a seminar paper on natural symbols which helped me to form my interest. I record gratefully my husband's unflagging attempt to keep the argument on the track and thanks to Janet for helping with the bibliography.

Mary Douglas
July 1969

*

Many difficulties and sources of confusion still remain in this Pelican edition. To try to unify so many fields of anthropology was a very ambitious task. Clearly another ten years of scholarly research would have made it more presentable. However, events move faster than study can. If this exercise in comparative cosmology has any relevance for the way we justify our own behaviour, it should be set forth with the least delay. Once made public, the weakness of the argument, step by step and example by example, could be criticized. The thesis was too complex to unfold in less space, too difficult to discuss piecemeal without laying down the whole, and too difficult to work out further in private study. Therefore, I published it when I did and wish to acknowledge my gratitude for the painstaking criticisms it has received. Particularly Professor Robin Horton, Professor Philip Gulliver, Dr Deane Neubauer and Mr Michael Thompson have been most constructive. I wish also to thank Professor Thomas Luckmann for encouraging me to make a revised edition at once and for his suggestions about how to set about it. It will be apparent that I have not been able to avail myself of all the helpful criticisms. The main difference between the two editions is the attempt to clarify the central dimensions of 'grid and group' on which the rest hangs. Instead of indicating a separate quadrant for each type of society, I am now thinking of scatter patterns across the diagram to show the group pressures and the coherence of the classificatory scheme which can be assessed from ethnography or historical biography. If the reasoning is sound, we can go a great deal further than the phenomenologists who have been saying for some time that the perceived universe is socially constructed. We should be able to say what kinds of universe are likely to be constructed when social relations take this or that form.

Now that Professor Bernstein's essay on the *Classification and Framing of Educational Knowledge* (1971) is published, my book shows up more obviously as the other side of his thesis. This meets a criticism from those who felt I had not fully explained the relevance of his work to my ideas. The revised grid and group is derived from his discussion of the ways the curriculum can be constructed. He has been interested in revealing how speech forms, and now the curriculum, encode the pattern of social relations, mediate and reinforce it. Any given curriculum is justified by a cosmology which states the ultimate principles in the universe, and which derives from these principles the proper way to teach human beings. As he looks beneath the curriculum to the pattern of power which is being hammered out in bargaining over the staff-meeting table, so I try to look beneath the overt cosmology to the pattern of power which it realizes. And one step further, I have tried to identify with the type of cosmology and social pattern a distinctive coding of ritual forms. The coding of ritual forms corresponds to the coding of speech forms in Basil Bernstein's earlier work. The curriculum is seen as a system of boundaries: likewise the tribal culture. His study of the curriculum examines the main varieties which differ in the strength of the boundaries used. The difference between strong boundary maintenance and weak boundary maintenance in education is analogous to the difference between ritual and anti-ritual in types of religion. This theme of the variable strength of the boundaries of cognitive systems I was forced to explore after writing

Purity and Danger (1966). For in that study I emphasized the communication function of all boundings of experience, without facing the empirical fact that some societies persist very well without strongly bounded cognitive categories and some tolerate anomaly more easily than others. *Natural Symbols* is an attempt to answer questions raised by myself from the programme of the earlier book.

Basil Bernstein says of the curriculum that it is a scheme for fitting together bits of knowledge. As they are connected in the curriculum so they enter the minds of the pupils, and, though the details of the content will fade, the connections are likely to guide their judgements and perpetuate the system of power which the curriculum represents. This feedback, which gives stability to educational systems, also stabilizes cosmologies. The cosmological scheme connects up the bits of experience and invests the whole with meaning; the people who accept it will only be able to justify their treatment of one another in terms of these ultimate categories. Unless we can make the process visible, we are the victims.

Mary Douglas
December 1971

Introduction

The title of this book would seem to hold a contradiction. Nature must be expressed in symbols; nature is known through symbols which are themselves a construction upon experience, a product of mind, an artifice or conventional product, therefore the reverse of natural. Nor can there be sense in speaking of natural symbols unless the mind tends in some natural way to use the same symbols for the same situations. This question through the ages has been deeply explored and the possibility of natural symbols is rejected. A symbol only has meaning from its relation to other symbols in a pattern. The pattern gives the meaning. Therefore no one item in the pattern can carry meaning by itself isolated from the rest. Therefore even the human physiology which we all share in common does not afford symbols which we can all understand. A cross-cultural, pan-human pattern of symbols must be an impossibility. For one thing, each symbolic system develops autonomously according to its own rules. For another, cultural environments add their difference. For another, the social structures add a further range of variation. The more closely we inspect the conditions of human interaction, the more unrewarding if not ridiculous the quest for natural symbols appears. However, the intuition against such a learned negative is strong. This book attempts to reinstate the intuition by following the line of argument of the French sociologists of *L'Année sociologique*. For if it is true, as they asserted, that the social relations of men provide the prototype for the logical relations between things, then, whenever this prototype falls into a common pattern, there should be something common to be discerned in

11

the system of symbols it uses. Where regularities in the system are found, we should expect to find recurring, and always intelligible across cultures, the same natural systems of symbols. Society was not simply a model which classificatory thought followed; it was its own divisions which served as divisions for the system of classification. The first logical categories were social categories; the first classes of things were classes of men into which these things were integrated. It was because men were grouped and thought of themselves in the form of groups that in their ideas they grouped other things. The centre of the first scheme of nature is not the individual; it is society (Durkheim and Mauss, 1903: 82, 87). The quest for natural symbols becomes by the force of this argument the quest for natural systems of symbolizing. We will look for tendencies and correlations between the character of the symbolic system and that of the social system.

The easiest to recognize of these tendencies can be expressed as the rule of distance from physiological origin. I have argued elsewhere (in *Purity and Danger*, 1966) that the organic system provides an analogy of the social system which, other things being equal, is used in the same way and understood in the same way all over the world. The body is capable of furnishing a natural system of symbols, but our problem is to identify the elements in the social dimension which are reflected in one view and another of how the body should function or how its waste-products should be judged. In that book I made some suggestions, but the subject is very complex. According to the rule of distance from physiological origin (or the purity rule) the more the social situation exerts pressure on persons involved in it, the more the social demand for conformity tends to be expressed by a demand for physical control. Bodily processes are more ignored and more firmly set outside the social discourse, the more the latter is important. A natural way of investing a social occasion with dignity is to hide organic processes. Thus social distance tends to be expressed in distance from physiological origins and vice versa.

Maimonides, the twelfth-century Jewish philosopher, explains the anthropomorphic reference to God in this idiom. Organs of locomotion or of sensation or of speech are figuratively ascribed to God, to express his agency in certain results. The Lord has a powerful voice (Psalms xxiv, 4), his tongue is a devouring fire (Isaiah xx, 27), his eyes behold (Psalms ii, 4). The external organs have a straightforward figurative sense, since power to act and to know are among God's attributes. But a problem arises when internal organs have to be interpreted:

In phrases like 'my bowels are troubled for him' (Jeremiah xxxi, 20); 'The sounding of thy bowels' (Isaiah lxiii, 15), the term 'bowels' is used in the sense of 'heart'; for the term 'bowels' is used both in a general and in a specific meaning; it denotes specifically 'bowels' but more generally it can be used as the name of any inner organ, including 'heart'. The correctness of this argument can be proved by the phrase 'And thy law is within my bowels' (Psalms xl, 9), which is identical with 'And thy law is within my heart'. For that reason the prophet employed in this verse the phrase 'my bowels are troubled' (and 'the sounding of thy bowels'); the verb *hamah* is in fact used more frequently in connection with 'heart' than with any other organ; compare 'My heart maketh a noise (*homeh*) in me' (Jeremiah iv, 19). Similarly, the shoulder is never used as a figure in reference to God, because it is known as a mere instrument of transport, and also comes into close contact with the thing which it carries. With far greater reason the organs of nutrition are never attributed to God; they are at once recognized as signs of imperfection.

The possibility of imagining God with organs of digestion and excretion is out of the question for this divine. Indeed it is not entertained at all for the Jewish religion. But this is not a universal tendency. Many religions worship gods who are incarnate in every sense. The Incarnation is the central, distinctive doctrine of Christianity. A basic question for understanding natural symbolic systems will be to know what social conditions are the prototype for the one or the other set of attitudes to the human body and its fitness or unfitness for figuring godhead. What are the limits within which the disdain of organic processes can be used as an idiom for social distance? Great methodological difficulties are encountered in any attempt to answer these questions.

One of the most intractable difficulties is the problem of holding other variables steady while we compare a piece of behaviour in one culture with a parallel one in another. Take the case of laughter, for instance. In any of a number of social systems the idea of loud vociferous laughter may be unseemly in polite company. But what counts as loud and vociferous may vary greatly. In her *Book of Manners for Women* (1897, p. 12) Mrs Humphry described rather unkindly the laughter of a theatre audience of whom very few 'know how to indulge themselves in the expression of their mirth'.

For every one whose laughter is melodious, there will be found a dozen who merely grin and half-a-dozen whose sole relief is in physical contortion. Some of the latter bend forward, folding themselves almost double, then spring back again, and repeat this jerky and ridiculous movement at every joke. Others throw their heads back in a way that disagreeably suggests dislocation. A few are so put to it to give vent to their overwhelming sense of amusement that they violently slap themselves, twisting about the whole as though they were undergoing tortures. Cachinnations in every key resound on all sides, varying from the shrill and attenuated 'He! he!' to the double chuckle 'Ho! ho!' fired off like postmen's knocks, at a tremendous speed, so as to be ready, decks cleared, for the next joke. Cackling suggestive of the farmyard, and snorts not unreminiscent of pig-styes, produce variety.

Mrs Humphry disapproved of dislocation, violence, jerks, uncontrolled cachinnations, snorts and cackles. In a chapter on learning to laugh, she stated: 'There is no greater ornament to conversation than the ripple of silvery notes that forms the perfect laugh.' But what passes for a ripple in one culture can be taken for a series of uncouth jerks in another. This is the central problem of comparison that has shackled the attempt to compare rules of bodily behaviour between different societies or different historical periods of the same people. If we are trying to compare forms of expression, we are involved in assessing behaviour in the physical dimension. The range of physical variables is so astonishingly great that it obviously contains a large cultural element. As Lévi-Strauss has said:

The thresholds of excitement, the limits of resistance are different in each culture. The 'impossible' effort, the 'unbearable' pain, the 'unbounded' pleasure are less individual functions than criteria sanctioned by collective approval, and disapproval. Each technique, each item of behaviour, traditionally learnt and transmitted, is based on certain nervous and muscular syndromes which constitute true systems, related within a total sociological context. (1950: xii)

It fc"..... that no objective physiological limits to the range from most complete bodily control to most utter abandonment are relevant. Similarly for all the possible range of symbolic expressions: each social environment sets its own limits to the modes of expression. From London to the north standard stimulants shift from beer to whisky, between some social circles they shift from weak tea to coffee, to shandy. And with these shifts go special ranges of noise and quiet, and of bodily gesture. There is no way of controlling the cultural differences. And yet, without some method, the cross-cultural comparison falls to the ground and with it the whole interest of this exercise. If we cannot bring the argument back from tribal ethnography to ourselves, there is little point in starting it at all. The same goes for the experience of social control. What it feels like to have other people controlling one's behaviour varies with the quality of restraints and freedoms they can use. Each social environment sets limits to the possibilities of remoteness or nearness of other humans, and limits the costs and rewards of group allegiance and conformity to social categories. To compare across cultures is like trying to compare the worth of primitive currencies where no common standard of value applies. And yet the problem is basically the same as that faced by linguists in comparing tonal languages in which the variations in tone occur within a range of relative pitch and not in relation to absolute pitch. One way to solve the comparative problem is to limit the predictions of a hypothesis to any given social environment. Even here the difficulty of defining a social environment is great. The methodological rule is merely a rough kind of safeguard against the wildest kinds of cultural selections.

It serves to counter the effects of Bongo-Bongoism, the trap of all anthropological discussion. Hitherto when a generalization is tentatively advanced, it is rejected out of court by any field-workers who can say: 'This is all very well, but it doesn't apply to the Bongo-Bongo.' To enter this present discussion the Bongoist must precisely specify the cultural field within which his comparisons are drawn.

The hypothesis which I will propose about concordance be-tween symbolic and social experience will always have to be tested within a given social environment. One of the arguments will be that the more value people set on social constraints, the more the value they set on symbols of bodily control. The rule of comparison will not allow me to compare Lloyd George's unruly hair with Disraeli's flowing locks, for they belonged to different cultural periods in English history. Strictly it should not allow me to compare Lloyd George with a younger generation of more close-cropped contemporaries. The latitude allowed by the term 'given social environment' is a matter of discretion. The more limited the cultural ranges within which the comparison is made, the more significant the results.

Bearing these rules of method in mind, I will try to identify four distinctive systems of natural symbols. These will be social systems in which the image of the body is used in different ways to reflect and enhance each person's experience of society. According to one, the body will tend to be conceived as an organ of communication. The major preoccupations will be with its functioning effectively; the relation of head to subordinate members will be a model of the central control system, the favour-ite metaphors of statecraft will harp upon the flow of blood in the arteries, sustenance and restoration of strength. According to another, though the body will also be seen as a vehicle of life, it will be vulnerable in different ways. The dangers to it will come not so much from lack of co-ordination or of food and rest, but from failure to control the quality of what it absorbs through the orifices; fear of poisoning, protection of boundaries, aversion to bodily waste products and medical theory that enjoins fre-quent purging. Another again will be very practical about the possible uses of bodily rejects, very cool about recycling waste matter and about the pay-off from such practices. The distinction between the life within the body and the body that carries it will hold no interest. In the control areas of this society controversies about spirit and matter will scarcely arise. But at the other end of the spectrum, where the vast majority are controlled by these pragmatists, a different attitude will be seen. Here the body is not primarily the vehicle of life, for life will be seen as purely spiritual, and the body as irrelevant matter. Here we can locate millennial tendencies from our early history to the present day. For these people, society appears as a system which does not work. The human body is the most readily available image of a system. In these types of social experience, a person feels that his personal relations, so inexplicably unprofitable, are in the sinister grip of a social system. It follows that the body tends to serve as a symbol of evil, as a structured system contrasted with pure spirit which by its nature is free and undifferentiated. The millennialist is not interested in identifying enemies and disabling them. He believes in a Utopian world in which goodness of heart can prevail without institutional devices. He does not seek to cherish any particular social forms. He would sweep them all away. The millennialist goes in for frenzies; he welcomes the letting-go experience, and incorporates it into his procedure for bringing in the millennium. He seeks bodily ecstasy which, by expressing for him the explosive advent of the new age, reaffirms the value of the doctrine. Philosophically his bias is towards distinguishing spirit from flesh, mind from matter. But for him the flesh does not suggest temptation to lust and all physical delights. It would more likely represent the corruption of power and organization. For him spirit is found working freely in nature and in the spirit of the wild – not in society. By this avenue of thought anthropologists can relate their field material to the traditional subject matter of the history of religions. For it uncovers implicit forms of the great theological controversies. According to some religions gods and men can have sexual intercourse; in others too great a barrier separates them; in others the god can take human form, only in appearance, not in the reality of flesh; in others the god is incarnate, but not by the normal physiological process. Here we have an index, as Leach has pointed out in discussing dogmas of virgin birth, of the way in which spirit and matter are categorized. For some people the categories are very distinct and it is blasphemous to mix them, for others the mixing of divine and human is right and normal. But I hope to show that dimensions of social life govern the fundamental attitudes to spirit and matter.

1   Away from Ritual

One of the gravest problems of our day is the lack of commitment to common symbols. If this were all, there would be little to say. If it were merely a matter of our fragmentation into small groups, each committed to its proper symbolic forms, the case would be simple to understand. But more mysterious is a wide-spread, explicit rejection of rituals as such. Ritual is become a bad word signifying empty conformity. We are witnessing a revolt against formalism, even against form. 'The vast majority of my class-mates just sat through four years.' So wrote Newfield of what he called the ungeneration of his college year: 'They didn't challenge any authority, take any risks or ask any questions. They just memorized "the given", not even complaining when instructions turned them into mindless tape-recorders, demanding they recite rather than reason' (Newfield, 1966: 41). Shades of Luther! Shades of the Reformation and its complaint against meaningless rituals, mechanical religion, Latin as the language of cult, mind-less recitation of litanies. We find ourselves, here and now, re-living a world-wide revolt against ritualism. To understand it, Marx and Freud have been invoked, but Durkheim also foretold it and it behoves the social anthropologist to interpret alienation. Some of the tribes we observe are more ritualist than others. Some are more discontented than others with their traditional forms. From tribal studies there is something to say about a dimension which is usually ignored – the band or area of per-sonal relations in which an individual moves. But in trying to say it, we are handicapped by terminology.

Many sociologists, following Merton (1957: 131ff.), use the

term ritualist for one who performs external gestures without inner commitment to the ideas and values being expressed. Thus these apathetic students would be ritualists. There is some analogy in this to the usage of zoologists. For example, when an animal is said to make a ritual attack the zoologist means that a sequence of movements is initiated which, if completed normally, would end in aggression; the function of the animal ritual is communication, for when the other animal receives the signal, it changes its behaviour into ritual submission, thus inhibiting and checking the sequence of aggressive actions. This seems to be a perfectly legitimate way of distinguishing between symbolic and other behaviour in animals. A form of communication is identified; no judgement is implied about the value of the ritual as compared with other forms of communication. However, when this usage is transferred to human behaviour, ritual, defined as a routinized act diverted from its normal function, subtly becomes a despised form of communication. Other symbolic acts accurately convey information about the intentions and commitments of the actor: ritual does not. The ritualist becomes one who performs external gestures which imply commitment to a particular set of values, but he is inwardly withdrawn, dried out and uncommitted. This is a distractingly partisan use of the term. For it derives from the assumptions of the anti-ritualists in the long history of religious revivalism. The sociologist may maintain that the emotional legacy does not disturb his cool objectivity. He cannot deny however that it leaves him without convenient terminology for describing the other kind of symbolic action which correctly expresses the actor's internal state. It would be decidedly cumbrous to use anti-ritualism for the positively committed use of symbolic forms in order to keep ritualism in its pejorative, sectarian sense. There is another reason for using ritual in a neutral sense. Anthropologists need to communicate with sociologists as well as with zoologists. They are in the habit of using ritual to mean action and beliefs in the symbolic order without reference to the commitment or non-commitment of the actors. They have a practical reason for this usage. For in small-scale, face-to-face society the gulf between personal meanings and public meanings cannot develop; rituals are not fixed; discrepancy between the situation being enacted and the form of expression is immediately reduced by change in the latter. Primitive jurisprudence sees no gap between law and morality, because there are no written precedents and because small changes in the law can be constantly made to express new moral situations and because such changes, being unrecorded, are unperceived. The idea of an immutable God-given law is in practice compatible with a changing legal situation. If this is so in the formal situation of specialized tribal law courts, how much more so in the public use of religious symbols in primitive society. However earnestly the anthropologist is assured that the worship of the gods follows an immutable pattern from the beginning of tribal history, there is no justification whatever for believing what the performers themselves believe. Primitive religions are fortunate in that they cannot carry a dead weight of 'ritualized' ritual (to adopt the sociologist's usage). Therefore anthropologists have not needed so far to consider the difference between external symbolic forms and internal states. It is fair enough that 'ritualized' ritual should fall into contempt. But it is illogical to despise all ritual, all symbolic action as such. To use the word ritual to mean empty symbols of conformity, leaving us with no word to stand for symbols of genuine conformity, is seriously disabling to the sociology of religion. For the problem of empty symbols is still a problem about the relation of symbols to social life, and one which needs an unprejudiced vocabulary.

The anthropological usage relates the discussion more honestly to the historical controversies in religion. Ritual in the positive sense corresponds to ritualism in Church history, and allows us to identify ritualists and anti-ritualists in terms which they themselves would use. We are thus able to reflect upon ourselves and consider the causes of anti-ritualism today.

An instructive example is the recent concern of the Roman Catholic hierarchy in England with Friday abstinence. This is a rule which, on the one hand, is dear to large sections of the Catholic population. They adhere to it, confess its breach with contrition, generally take it seriously. On the other hand it is

21

not highly regarded by the clergy. In their eyes the avoidance of meat on Fridays has become an empty ritual, irrelevant to true religion. In this argument the anti-ritualists are the clergy and the ritualists a type known patronizingly as the Bog Irishmen. Bog Irishism seems to be a highly magical, irrational, non-verbal culture. Paradoxically the Bog Irish are found, not so much in Ireland, as in London parishes. Friday abstinence is the core rule of their religion: it is a taboo whose breach will bring automatic misfortune. It is the only sin they think worth mentioning in confession and they evidently believe that it will count against them more heavily on the day of judgement than breach of any of the ten commandments. To bring them nearer to the true doctrines, the rule of Friday abstinence has now been abolished in England and an active movement of new catechetics attempts to wean their offspring from magicality and bring them to a superior form of worship.

When I ask my clerical friends why the new forms are held superior, I am answered by a Teilhardist evolutionism which assumes that a rational, verbally explicit, personal commitment to God is self-evidently more evolved and better than its alleged contrary, formal, ritualistic conformity. Questioning this, I am told that ritual conformity is not a valid form of personal commitment and is not compatible with the full development of the personality; also that the replacement of ritual conformity with rational commitment will give greater meaning to the lives of Christians. Furthermore if Christianity is to be saved for future generations, ritualism must be rooted out, as if it were a weed choking the life of the spirit. We find in all this a mood which closely parallels the anti-ritualism which has inspired so many evangelical sects. There is no need to go back to the Reformation to recognize the wave on which these modern Catholics are rather incongruously riding.

Today, as much amongst us as the immigrant Irish, are the thriving, numerous Protestant sects which each arose in turn by rejecting ecclesiology, and by seeking to return to the primitive purity of the Gospel message, speaking straight to the heart of the worshipper without intervening ritual forms.

Is this move against ritual to be seen as a matter of swings of the pendulum? Such an approach implies that any strong impulse towards ritual must eventually be countered by an impulse in the other sense. One of the usual explanations of the regular renewal of anti-ritualism is that revolts against established hierarchical systems of religion come from the disinherited. A popular combination of Freud and Weber, it assumes that the principal religious function is to cope with psychological maladjustment and that as this function becomes more or less established, so the social forms become more or less routinized. A movement which begins as a sect expressing the religious needs of the poor gradually moves up the social scale. It becomes respectable. Its rituals increase, its rigorous fundamentalism in devotion to the Word becomes as weighted with magic as the sacramental edifice it started by denying. With respectability comes ritualism. With loss of good fortune comes anti-ritualism and the new sect. This is the assumption underlying many of the contributions to *Patterns of Sectarianism* (ed. Wilson, 1967). Bryan Wilson expresses it very clearly himself when he offers a maladjustment theory for the development of anti-ritualist sects. Maladjustment is bound to follow from social change. Hence the impulse to new sects grows with the speed of change.

The specific factors of stimulus of sect emergence are usually found in the stresses and tensions differentially experienced within the total society. Change in the economic position of a particular group (which may be a change only in relative position); disturbance of normal social relations, for instance in the circumstances of industrialization and urbanization; the failure of the social system to accommodate particular age, sex and status groups – all of these are possible stimuli in the emergence of sects. These are the needs to which the sects, to some extent, respond. Particular groups are rendered marginal by some process of social change; there is a sudden need for a new interpretation of their social position, or for a transvaluation of their experience. Insecurity, differential status anxiety, cultural neglect, prompt a need for readjustment which sects may, for some, provide. (1967: 31)

And so on.

23

The argument which seeks to explain behaviour by reference to maladjustment, compensation, deprival is always fair game. When it rears its head among empirical sociologists it is a particularly pleasant duty to give chase. For the psychoanalysts, who popularized this equilibrium model of human nature, based their case on its therapeutic value. The question of forming scientifically verifiable propositions was not their primary concern. But for a sociologist to seek the origins of a class of religious movement in terms of maladjustment and readjustment is to abdicate his role. Either he must use the proposition to prove its own premise, or he must admit it is valueless for explaining negative instances. What about the Bog Irish? Are they not dispossessed, deprived, suffering disturbance of normal social relations? When they find themselves labouring in London, or, rather, queuing outside labour exchanges, do they not feel a sudden need for a new interpretation of their social experience? For what status could be more insecure, more marginal and anxiety-prone than that of the immigrant unskilled worker in London? Yet there they are, clinging tenaciously to their ancient ecclesiastical organization and elaborate ritualism from which far less obviously marginal and socially insecure preachers strive to dislodge them. We can be dissatisfied, therefore, with this as an explanation of anti-ritualism.

The deprivation hypothesis has its roots deep in our cultural heritage. Perhaps Rousseau gave the first and most emphatic vision of the individual enchained by society and liable to revolt after a certain pitch of humiliation and despair has been reached. The assumption that has bedevilled sociology ever since is that deprival and strain can be measured cross-culturally. In my Chapter 3 below I attempt to establish methodological limits within which these notions can be applied. Anyone who uses the idea of strain or stress in a general explanatory model is guilty, at the very least, of leaving his analysis long before it is complete, at worst, of circularity. Smelser, for example, puts the factor of strain into his explanation of mass movements, panics, crazes and religious movements. Strain, for him, results from discontinuity between roles and performance (Smelser, 1962 : 54), but as this discontinuity cannot be assessed he proceeds to postulate its emergence as a result of social change. He detects structural strain when large classes of unattached persons flood into towns, or equally in what he calls 'pinched' groups (op. cit.: 199 and 338). So we are little further in locating causes of mass movements of different kinds. The emotional content of a word like 'strain' inhibits analysis as much as maladjustment, deprivation, frustration and the rest. A further difficulty lies in concentrating on change and movement, for these can always be presumed to start in a state of disequilibrium. It is more revealing to identify in certain kinds of collective action both the distinctive social structure and the correlated symbolism which are found in the steady state in some small-scale primitive societies.

Even amongst ourselves, there is a long-term tendency to be reckoned with. A trend towards unritualistic forms of worship is found not merely among the dispossessed and disoriented. Contemporary Catholicism in America displays an

individual emphasis, found also in Protestant spirituality, focuses on a personal type of religious experience in which the individual considers himself and God to the relative exclusion of his neighbour.

For those who get their spirituality in the form of reading, the sociologist of religion goes on to say,

the bulk of spiritual reading recommended to Catholics for two centuries has emphasized this private spirituality . . . In Gospel language, this means that the role of Mary took . . . precedence over that of Martha. (Neal, 1965: 26–7)

Let me use this excerpt to signpost three phases in the move away from ritualism. First, there is the contempt of external ritual forms; second, there is the private internalizing of religious experience; third, there is the move to humanist philanthropy. When the third stage is under way, the symbolic life of the spirit is finished. For each of these stages social determinants can be identified. Loyalty to my Bog Irish ancestors would not in itself lead me to defend ritualism. Without being Irish, any anthropologist knows that public forms of symbolic expression are not to be despised. The reformers who set low value on the external

25

and symbolic aspects of Friday abstinence and who exhort the faithful to prefer elymosynary deeds are not making an intellectually free assessment of forms of worship. They are moving with the secular tide along with other sections of the middle classes who seek to be justified in their lives only by saving others from hunger and injustice. There are personal experiences which drive people in our society towards justification by good works. But at this point notice also that the Irishism which clings to ritual forms is itself also socially determined. The Friday abstainers are not free to follow their pastors in their wide-ranging philanthropy. For each person's religion has to do with himself and his own autonomous needs. There is a sad disjunction between the recognized needs of clergy, teachers, writers and the needs of those they preach, teach and write for.

I hope to disclose these social determinants by considering small-scale, primitive cultures. The problem in hand is the central problem of religious history and it amazes me that anthropological insights have not yet been systematically used to resolve it. So little has been done to extend the analysis across modern and primitive cultures that there is still no common vocabulary. Sacraments are one thing, magic another; taboos one thing, sin another. The first thing is to break through the spiky, verbal hedges that arbitrarily insulate one set of human experiences (ours) from another set (theirs). To make a start I shall take ritualism to signify heightened appreciation of symbolic action. This will be manifested in two ways: belief in the efficacy of instituted signs, sensitivity to condensed symbols. The first is the sacramental, and equally the magical, theology. I see no advantage for this discussion in making any distinction between magical and sacramental. I could be talking about an historic shift in Europe from an emphasis on ritual efficacy before the Reformation to an emphasis on spontaneous, commemorative rites. Or I could be referring to the variation in tribal religions from strong to weak beliefs in magical efficacy. Let it make no difference to the argument whether I use the word magic or sacrament.

Ritualism is most highly developed where symbolic action is

held to be most certainly efficacious. Between Catholic and Anglican celebrations of the Eucharist there is a shift from the emphasis on ritual efficacy in the first, to the emphasis on a commemorative rite in the second. This is a fine difference in the series (ranging from magical to unmagical ritual) whose social origins we are considering. The difference is perhaps most easily identified in attitudes to wrong-doing. Where symbols are highly valued and ritualism strong, then the idea of sin involves specific, formal acts of wrong-doing; where ritualism is weak, the idea of sin does not focus on specific external actions, but on internal states of mind: rituals of purification will not be so much in evidence.

Before I launch into a comparison of primitive religions, I must recall the delicacy of the line on which a sacramental religion rests. Sacraments, as I understand, are signs specially instituted to be channels of grace. The whole material world is held to be sacramental in the sense that material signs and channels of grace are everywhere, always available; but the sacraments are specially instituted. The Christian who approaches a sacrament must fulfil stipulated ritual conditions. If these, for one reason or another, cannot be met, he can have recourse to the more diffuse sources of grace. Instead of actually going through the instituted form of confession and absolution, he can make an inward 'act of contrition'; instead of Eucharistic communion he can make an 'act of spiritual communion'. The devotion to the sacraments, then, depends on a frame of mind which values external forms and is ready to credit them with special efficacy. It is such a general attitude which commits the ritualist to sacramental forms of worship. And vice versa, a lack of interest in external symbols would not be compatible with a cult of instituted sacraments. Many of the current attempts to reform the Christian liturgy suppose that, as the old symbols have lost their meaning, the problem is to find new symbols or to revivify the meaning of the old ones. This could be a total waste of effort if, as I argue, people at different historic periods are more or less sensitive to signs as such. Some people are deaf or blind to non-verbal signals. I argue that the perception of symbols in general, as well as their interpretation, is socially determined. If I can establish this, it will be important for the criticism of maladjustment or strain theories of religious behaviour.

First, to dispose of the popular idea that all primitive religions are magical and taboo-ridden. Robertson Smith voiced this impression that there has been, through the centuries, a progressive decline of magic accompanying the growth of civilization. He was not altogether wrong. But the great secular movement he describes, if it is not an optical illusion, at least has been frequently interrupted. Among primitive cultures far removed from industrial progress we find non-ritualists.

Ritualism is taken to be a concern that efficacious symbols be correctly manipulated and that the right words be pronounced in the right order. When we compare the sacraments to magic there are two kinds of view to take into account: on the one hand the official doctrine, on the other the popular forms it takes. On the first view the Christian theologian may limit the efficacy of sacraments to the internal working of grace in the soul. But by this agency external events may be changed, since decisions taken by a person in a state of grace will presumably differ from those of others. Sacramental efficacy works internally: magical efficacy works externally. But this difference, even at the theological level, is less great than it seems. For if the theologian remembers to take account of the doctrine of the Incarnation, magical enough in itself, and the even more magical doctrine of the Resurrection and of how its power is channelled through the sacraments, he cannot make such a tidy distinction between sacramental and magical efficacy. Then there is the popular magicality in Christianity. A candle lit to St Anthony for finding a lost object is magical, as also a St Christopher medal used to prevent accidents or the expectation that meat eaten on a Friday would bring one out in spots. Both sacramental and magical behaviour are expressions of ritualism. What we learn about the conditions in which magic thrives or declines in primitive cultures should apply to sacramentalism among ourselves and should apply equally to the turning away from magic and ritual which was expressed in the Protestant Reformation.

The advantage of taking belief in efficacious signs as the focus of the comparison is that other aspects of religious behaviour largely coincide with variations on this score. I have mentioned how ideas of sin tend to vary with ideas of magicality. The concept of formal transgression can take on a very magical aspect indeed, and again, the more magicality, the more sensitive the perception of condensed symbols. All communication depends on use of symbols, and they can be classified in numerous ways, from the most precise to the most vague, from single reference signs to multi-reference symbols. I ask you here to be interested in a variation, within the class of multi-reference symbols, which runs from the most diffuse to the most condensed. For examples of highly condensed symbols, read Turner's interpretation of Ndembu rituals. This people in Zambia experiences human society as a complex structure of descent groups and local groups stratified by age and cult associations. To symbolize this they fasten on the colours of the juices in the human body and in the earth and trees. The active principles in humans are black bile, red blood and white milk; in the world of living nature there are trees with milky saps and red, sticky resins and charred black wood; likewise, minerals include black earth, white and red clay. From these colours they work out a complex representation of male and female spheres, and destructive and nourishing powers, interlocking at more and more abstract and inclusive levels of interpretation. So economical and highly articulated is this system of signs that it is enough to strike one chord to recognize that the orchestration is on a cosmic scale (Turner, 1968). For Christian examples of condensed symbols, consider the sacraments, particularly the Eucharist and the Chrisms. They condense an immensely wide range of reference summarized in a series of statements loosely articulated to one another. By contrast, for diffuse symbols, take as an example the Mbuti pygmies' word for 'joy', described by Turnbull as the focusing element of their system of values, or the words 'human values' in contemporary BBC culture. The ideas are comprehensive enough in reference; they produce a standard emotional response. But it is difficult to analyse their connotation precisely. I am suggesting that the rule

29

of Friday abstinence is a minor condensed symbol for the exiled Irish in London, as abstinence from pork has become a symbol of the Law for Jews everywhere. Some English Catholics and Jews feel no response to these condensed symbols and are more moved by general ethical principles. My hypothesis is that these responses are respectively aspects of particular kinds of social experience. Implicitly I find myself returning to Robertson Smith's idea that rites are prior and myths are secondary in the study of religion. For it would seem that the recent shifts in Christian doctrine which are taking place in the long theological debate since the Reformation are attempts to bring intellectual positions into line with deeply imprinted, personal attitudes to ritualism. A full development of this argument should enable us to assess the social context of anti-ritualist movements and of their periodic defeat by ritualism.

At the present stage of ethnographic reporting it is not reliable enough a basis for comparison to look for the presence or absence of condensed symbols. For there is the nagging possibility that if a fieldworker of the calibre of Victor Turner or Raymond Firth went to the pygmies and carried out his customarily intensive investigation, he would discover as condensed a set of symbols as any on the seven hills of Rome. Some symbolic scheme of orientations may be necessary for people to relate to one another in time and space. This would not in itself necessarily mean that their beliefs take on a sacramental form. Since I am developing a sociological approach to the problem, let me concentrate, not on the other characteristics of the belief system, but only on the kind of use to which people put their symbols in everyday life, as regulators or as channels of power. That is, we should attend more to their ideas about ritual efficacy, and less to the structure of their orientations.

Take first the case of a tribe whose traditional religion was magical, and where a sizable minority switched to a Protestant-like reform of ritual and conscience. David Aberle writes:

The traditional Navaho fears error in his rituals and particularly error in the fixed prayers which chanter and patient must repeat in the course of a ceremony. Error may not only render the ceremony ineffec-

tual but may cause illness to the patient years later . . . Navaho supernatural power is likely to harm man when man breaches various
taboos, but these taboos have almost nothing to do with the moral
order. If a man were to commit murder, he might have ghost trouble –
but so might he if he worked in a hospital or happened to burn wood
from a hogan where someone had died. His ghost trouble stems from
ritual contamination, not from God's curse or the ghost's vengeance.
Theft, adultery, deceit, assault and rape have no supernatural
sanctions . . . True, ceremonies are impaired if the singer becomes
angry or if there is quarrelling at the ceremony. In this sense there are
supernatural sanctions against misbehaviour – but only while the
ceremony continues. On the other hand, the Navaho must fear the
consequences of many accidental breaches of taboos. (1966)

From this position of extreme ritualism a large minority of
Navaho have adopted a religion centred on the ritual eating of
peyote. The religion of the peyotists differs utterly from the traditional one, in their ritual, their ideas of sin and of God. The
peyotists value spontaneity in their prayers and insist there is no
fixed pattern in them. As Aberle puts it,

The traditional Navaho tries to bind power by formulae while the
peyotist tries to sway God by his fervour.

The peyotists' God is interested in morality. Confession of sin is
necessary to gain God's blessing and aid.

Full details of this religious change are given in David Aberle's
remarkable book. Here I need only indicate the change in social
conditions which accompanied the change of religious worship.
Navaho life was based on sheepherding in very arid, difficult
conditions, mainly in Arizona and New Mexico. A man with
many sheep used to gather round him other families who man-
aged portions of his herd for him and in return were given part
of the yield. These units must have been extremely cohesive, the
basis for economic aid in crises and for revenge and moral control.

The largest organized unit of Navaho kinship was a group of local
matrilineal kinsmen who actually co-operated and assisted one another
on a day to day and year to year basis . . . A man might lose his accumulated wealth through a bad winter or a dry summer. Hence an

31

ethic of sharing was general, with primary dependency on matrilineal kin but secondary dependence on many other kinsmen as well, including affines. The wealthy were supposed to be generous, the poor unremitting in their pressures for generosity. Mutuality among kinsmen was reinforced by . . . the process of regulating disputes: here self help and compensation were the rule. A headman could only arbitrate, and kinsmen were needed for support in case of feud, pressure for compensation or need to pay compensation. (ibid.: 44)

How tight this community life was and what strong controls to conform were exerted by the sanctions of reciprocity in hardship may be seen from the attitude to moral rules. European inquirers were apparently surprised to find that Navaho ethical standards were supported not by love of virtue but by fear of reprisals, fear of withdrawal of support and fear of shame. Aberle's book is a documented study of the gradual breakdown of the basis of community moral control. American law and order substituted for vengeance groups.

Clan cohesion was impaired as the possibility of mutual aid was reduced. Fear of loss of support in the community also became a lesser threat. And fear of loss of face or shame depends on the degree of involvement in the face-to-face community. Not only was intra-community interdependence lessened and enforcement of morality impaired, but extra-community dependence on wage work, and familial economic autonomy, was increased . . . (ibid.: 200–201)

This one example suggests that when the social group grips its members in tight communal bonds, the religion is ritualist; when this grip is relaxed, ritualism declines. And with this shift of forms, a shift in doctrines appears. The social experience of the traditional Navaho man conditioned him to automatic response to his community's demands. Abstract right or wrong, internal motives, these were much less important to him than knowing to which vengeance group he belonged and to whom he was bound in a web of reciprocities. But the new Navaho, impoverished by enforced de-stocking, inadequately involved in the American wage and cash economy, had to learn to discriminate between the obligatory claims of his family and optional claims of charity. Private judgement controlled his behaviour, not blind loyalty. He could not count on his kinsmen, nor should they on him. He was alone. Eating peyote gave him a sense of greatly enhanced personal worth and a sense of direct communion with the supernatural. Notice that his God has become like himself, no more coerced by powerful symbols of reciprocity and allegiance. He judges intentions and capacities. He does not apply fixed rules automatically but pierces behind the symbolic façade to judge the inner heart of man. God has turned against ritual. Here is a fascinating small-scale model of the Protestant Reformatio⊓, well worth exploring further. I shall return to the Navaho pey⊓tist again. But as their anti-ritualism is a response to modern c⊓nditions, it does not satisfy my need for primitive models.

F⊓ ⌐⌐.se I turn to an African study, Colin Turnbull's on the pygmies of the Ituri forest. From this I derive my initial thesis that the most important determinant of ritualism is the experience of closed social groups.

The pygmies represent the extreme case. So little ritual do they perform that their first ethnographers assumed that they had, to all intents and purposes, no religion, no culture even, of their own. All that they had was borrowed from the Bantu. Turnbull's work is inspired by the need to assert that their very lack of ritual is an aspect of an independent culture of their own. He draws a picture of pygmies, irreverently mocking solemn Bantu rites into which they have been drawn, uncomprehending the magic for hunting and fertility which their Bantu neighbours offer them, overcome with giggling during Bantu attempts to divine for sorcerers, quite unconcerned about incurring pollution of death. They perform no cult for the dead, they reject the Bantu idea of sin. The whole paraphernalia of Bantu religion is alien to them. Seen from the Bantu point of view they are ignorant, and irreligious. But they do not have any alternative set of paraphernalia, equally elaborate and imposing, but different. Their religion is one of internal feeling, not of external sign. The moods of the forest manifest the moods of the deity, and the forest can be humoured by the same means as the pygmies, by song and dance. Their religion is not concerned with their correct orientation within elaborate cosmic categories nor with acts of transgression, nor rules of purity; it is concerned with joy (1965: 289). It is a religion of faith, not works, to use an ancient slogan.

As to their social groupings – so fluid and so fluctuating is the band that a given territory witnesses 'a continual flux of individuals' (1965: 109). Bantu farmers consider that certain pygmies are attached to their villages by hereditary right and would very much like to know their whereabouts. But, Turnbull says:

> So with every lineage, as with every individual, there is an infinity of territories to which he may move if it pleases him, and the system, such as it is, encourages such movement to the point that no (Bantu) villager can ever be sure of what Mbuti lineages are hunting in 'his' territory. (1965: 109)

A camp of net hunters moves its site roughly every month. During that time newcomers are arriving and original members moving out, so that the composition is not the same throughout the month. Seven men are needed for the hunting season, and a camp of over twenty huts is counted as a large one. In the honey season such camps fragment into much smaller units.

> The pygmies seem bound by few set rules. There was a general pattern of behaviour to which everyone more or less conformed, but with great latitude given and taken. (1961: 80)

In such a society a man can hardly need to be preoccupied with the formalities of social intercourse. If a quarrel arises, he can easily move away. Loyalties are for the short term. Techniques of conciliation need not be elaborate or publicly instituted. I am not merely saying that the people's behaviour to their god corresponds to their behaviour to each other, though the truism could well be underlined. I am saying that religious forms as well as social forms are generated by experiences in the same dimension. Pygmies move freely in an uncharted, unsystematized, unbounded social world. I maintain that it would be impossible for them to develop a sacramental religion, as it would be im-

possible for the neighbouring Bantu farmers, living in their confined villages in forest clearings, to give up magic.

We can have confidence in the pygmy example because of the
obviously high quality of the ethnography. If Turnbull had been
careless, left gaps, seemed not to be aware of the implications of
what he has observed, if he had not followed up his statements
with such a wealth of secondary material, pygmy religion would
be of no interest. The same value attaches to studies of Nuer
and Dinka, pastoralists in the Sudan. I shall say more in Chapter
6 about these peoples. As far as religious behaviour goes, neither
tribe seems to be as Low Church as the pygmies. Yet their ethnographers have both had trouble, when asserting the non-ritualist
quality of their worship, in convincing their colleagues that a
tendency to idealize has not distorted their reporting. This is the
fate of every ethnographer who tries to describe an unritualist,
primitive religion. I have never known what to reply to anthropologists who have suggested that his own religious affiliations
may have coloured Professor Evans-Pritchard's interpretation of
Nuer religion (1956). I have heard them question Nuer disregard
of fetishism, alleged to be a foreign new importation (1956: 99).
As for the Nuer God, his intimacy with his worshippers, his
refusal to be coerced by sacrifice, his aptness for being described
in Christian theological forms, how far he seemed from the
traditional gods of primitive religions. Similarly for the God of
the Dinka (Lienhardt, 1961: 54, 73). I have even wondered
whether Robin Horton was perhaps justified in chiding Godfrey
Lienhardt for playing down the magical content of Dinka ritual
behaviour.

There is an occasional failure to call a spade a spade. For instance,
though it seems clear from the material offered that the Dinka think
certain actions symbolizing desired ends really do help in themselves to
achieve those ends, the author seems at times to want to rationalize
this magical element away. (1962: 78)

The book thus reviewed draws a very subtle, delicate line
between the expressive and efficacious functions of Dinka ritual.
In my view, Lienhardt offers a brilliant insight into the way in

which symbolic action controls experience. But is he guilty at the same time of overplaying the expressive and underplaying the magical element? Robin Horton read the Dinka book from his perspective in the steamy mangrove swamps of the Niger Delta where local communities are closed in and where magic is indubitably magic. But magic may be less important in open savannah lands.

My considered view now is that magical rites are not the same the world over and that interest in magical efficacy varies with the strength of the social ties. Those who doubt the existence in their own right of primitive, unritualist religions are in the position of old Father Schebesta. He assumed that if pygmies had no ritual elaborations as magical and complex as those of the Bantu, it must be proof that a former pygmy cultural heritage had been lost. So the sceptics suggest that something of magicality has been lost in the reporting of Dinka and Nuer religions. They betray the assumption that all primitive religions are equally magical. The case of the pygmies and of the old and new Navaho provide a basis for asserting that there are unritualist primitive religions. The difficulties of the ethnographers of the Nuer and the Dinka in convincing colleagues that their rituals are not very magical suggest that there is a real dimension to be investigated along a series from high to low ritualism in primitive cultures.

Secularization is often treated as a modern trend, attributable to the growth of cities or to the prestige of science, or just to the breakdown of social forms. But we shall see that it is an age-old cosmological type, a product of a definable social experience, which need have nothing to do with urban life or modern science. Here it would seem that anthropology has failed to hold up the right reflecting mirror to contemporary man. The contrast of secular with religious has nothing whatever to do with the contrast of modern with traditional or primitive. The idea that primitive man is by nature deeply religious is nonsense. The truth is that all the varieties of scepticism, materialism and spiritual fervour are to be found in the range of tribal societies. They vary as much from one another on these lines as any chosen segments of London life. The illusion that all primitives are pious, credulous and subject to the teaching of priests or magicians has probably done even more to impede our understanding of our own civilization than it has confused the interpretations of archaeologists dealing with the dead past. Very differently, for example, would Harvey Cox surely have described the secular trends of today if he had realized how closely the following words parallel accounts of some New Guinea tribal beliefs.

> In the age of the secular city, the questions with which we concern ourselves tend to be mostly functional and operational. We wonder how power can be controlled and used responsibly. We ask how a reasonable international order can be fashioned out of the technological community into which we have been hurried. We worry about how the wizardry of medical science can be applied to the full without creating a world population constantly hovering on the brink of famine. These are pragmatic questions, and we are pragmatic men whose interest in religion is at best peripheral. (Cox, 1968: 93)

Secularism is not essentially a product of the city. Secular in the sense of this-worldly, secular in the sense of failing to transcend the meanings of everyday, secular in the sense of paying no heed to specialized religious institutions, there are secular tribal cultures. Until he grasps this fact, the anthropologist himself is at a loss to interpret his own material. When he comes across an irreligious tribe, he redoubles the vigour and subtlety of his inquiries. He tries to squeeze his information harder to make it yield that overall superstructure of symbolism which his analysis can relate all through the book to the social substructure, or he dredges for at very least something to put in a final chapter on religion. So thwarted in this exercise was Fredrik Barth when he studied a group of Persian nomads that he was finally driven to write a special appendix to clear himself of the possible charges of insensibility to religious behaviour or of superficiality in his research.

> The Basseri show a poverty of ritual activities which is quite striking in the field situation; what they have of ceremonies, avoidance customs and beliefs seem to influence or be expressed in very few of their actions.

37

What is more, the different elements of ritual do not seem closely connected or interrelated in a wider system of meanings; they give the impression of occurring without reference to each other or to important features of the social structure ... (Barth, 1964, Appendix: 135)

The Basseri would apparently endorse this view, as they see themselves as slack Moslems, 'generally uninterested in religion as preached by Persian mullahs, and indifferent to metaphysical problems'. Good marks to Barth for so frankly recording his own surprise and professional frustration. He tries to solve the problem which still remains (because of his assumption that tribal society must have a straight Durkheimian religious expression) by trying to refine the conceptual tools of analysis: he has been led to look for expressive action specialized and apart from instrumental action; can it be possible that the distinction is not always valuable? Perhaps the symbolic meanings are implicit in the instrumental action, and that for the Basseri the meanings and values which make up their life are fully expressed in the richly dramatic sequence of their migrations: '... this value is not in fact expressed by means of technically unnecessary symbolic acts and exotic paraphernalia ... the migration cycle is used as a primary scheme for the conceptualization of time and space'. He suggests rather weakly after this that meanings can be implicit in the sequence of activities because of the 'picturesque and dramatic character of these activities, which makes of their migrations an engrossing and satisfying experience' (Barth : 153). The criterion of picturesqueness, however, would be difficult to apply to similar phenomena in urban America, even were it to fit pig-feasting in New Guinea. The meanings of the migration may well be expressed implicitly in the migration itself, but this says nothing about the meanings of society. Should not one suppose that a society which does not need to make explicit its representation of itself to itself is a special type of society? This would lead straight to what Barth says of the independence and self-sufficiency of the Basseri nomadic household which, enabling it to survive 'in economic relation with an external market but in complete isolation from all fellow nomads, is a very striking and fundamental feature of Basseri organization' (Barth: 21). These features will become more prominent as an explanation of secularity as my approach to the question is developed in this book. For one of the most obvious forms of religious behaviour, which Barth was looking for and failed to find, is the use of bodily symbols to express the notion of an organic social system. But it would seem that unless the form of personal relations corresponds in some obvious way to the form or functions of the body, a range of metaphysical questions of passionate interest to some people becomes entirely irrelevant.

2   To Inner Experience

Those on the New Left who are in revolt against empty rituals do not readily see themselves walking in the footprints of Wycliffe and of ardent Protestant reformers. Yet if we can make the leap from small exotic cultures to our European religious tradition, we can make the easier transition between anti-ritualism in a secular and in a religious context. We are then able to see that alienation from the current social values usually takes a set form: a denunciation not only of irrelevant rituals, but of ritualism as such; exaltation of the inner experience and denigration of its standardized expressions; preference for intuitive and instant forms of knowledge; rejection of mediating institutions, rejection of any tendency to allow habit to provide the basis of a new symbolic system. In its extreme forms anti-ritualism is an attempt to abolish communication by means of complex symbolic systems. We will see, as this argument develops, that it is a viable attitude only in the early, unorganized stages of a new movement. After the protest stage, once the need for organization is recognized, the negative attitude to rituals is seen to conflict with the need for a coherent system of expression. Then ritualism re-asserts itself around the new context of social relations. Fundamentalists, who are not magical in their attitude to the Eucharist, become magical in their attitude to the Bible. Revolutionaries who strike for freedom of speech adopt repressive sanctions to prevent return to the Tower of Babel. But each time this movement of revolt and anti-ritualism gives way to a new recognition of the need to ritualize, something has been lost from the original cosmic ordering of symbols. We arise from the purging of old rituals, simpler and poorer, as was intended, ritually beggared, but with other losses. There is a loss of articulation in the depth of past time. The new sect goes back as far as the primitive church, as far as the first Pentecost, or as far as the Flood, but the historical continuity is traced by a thin line. Only a narrow range of historical experience is recognized as antecedent to the present state. Along with celebrating the Last Supper with the breaking of bread, or the simplicity of fishermen-apostles, there is a squeamish selection of ancestors: just as revolutionaries may evict kings and queens from the pages of history, the anti-ritualists have rejected the list of saints and popes and tried to start again without any load of history.

But swings of the pendulum do not take us far enough in the interpretation of anti-ritualism. There is still the long secular trend to be accounted for which has resulted in a lack of sensitivity to condensed symbols, and at the same time a general preoccupation with lack of meaning. The move away from ritual is accompanied by a strong movement towards greater ethical sensitivity. Thus we find Christian denominations in the United States less and less distinguishable from one another and from the Jewish community, less and less willing to refer to doctrinal differences, and all equally committed to programmes of social betterment. This trend has been well described by Herberg in his *Protestant, Catholic, Jew* (1960) and documented by intensive research by Neal (1965). To understand it, however, I find myself drawn to the work of another sociologist whose research is specially relevant.

Ritual is pre-eminently a form of communication. Sociolinguistics provide us with an angle of approach. Basil Bernstein is a sociologist whose thought descends through Durkheim to Sapir (Bernstein, 1965: 148). His special concern is to discover how speech systems transform the experience of speakers. By a line of inquiry as subtle in its perception as it is powerful in scope he seeks to apply Sapir's insight about the controlling influence of language on culture.

It is quite an illusion to imagine that one adjusts to reality essentially without the use of language and that language is merely an incidental means of solving specific problems of communication or reflection. The fact of the matter is that the real world is to a large extent unconsciously built up on the language habits of the group ... We see and hear and otherwise experience very largely as we do because the language habits of our community predispose certain choices of interpretation. (Sapir, 1933: 155–69, quoted by Bernstein, op. cit., 1965)

This present book is an essay in applying Bernstein's approach to the analysis of ritual. It will help us to understand religious behaviour if we can treat ritual forms, like speech forms, as transmitters of culture, which are generated in social relations and which, by their selections and emphases, exercise a constraining effect on social behaviour. Even when we have summarized a little of what Bernstein has said, and then applied it to ritual as a medium of communication, we are still a long way from using his insights to understand anti-ritual. To this I hope to return in the last chapter.

Bernstein very cogently distinguishes his argument from that of Whorf and others who have treated language as an autonomous cultural agent and failed to relate its formal patterns to the structure of social relations. Indeed, before Bernstein it was difficult to see how such a relationship could be established. For certainly, in large areas of its internal development, language follows its own autonomously given rules. It is not surprising, as he has alleged (1965), that contemporary sociologists often seem to ignore the fact that humans speak, unless the sociologists are specially concerned with speech, in which case they emphasize its integrating or divisive functions. Speech tends to be treated as a datum, something taken for granted. If it is true that the analysis of speech as a social institution (one as basic as family and religion) has scarcely been broached, anthropologists are in no way to feel smug about the analysis of ritual. They do not make the mistake of neglecting this field; nor do they suppose that ritual is merely divisive or integrative in social relations. The data are piled up in great stacks of analysis of particular tribal symbolic systems which express the social order. But why some tribes should be pious and others irreverent or mercenary, why some are witch-ridden and others not, are questions which have only been entertained in sporadic fashion. As for the deeper question of whether symbolic forms are purely expressive, merely 'the means of solving specific problems of communication or reflection' as Sapir put it, or whether they interact on the social situations in which they arise, and whether their effect is constraining and reactionary – these questions are not systematically approached. Still less have anthropologists developed a frame of discourse in which their tribal studies can be related to ourselves. This is the point at which a revolutionary insight into language as a social process can help us.

Bernstein starts with the idea that there are two basic categories of speech, distinguishable both linguistically and sociologically. The first arises in a small-scale, very local social situation in which the speakers all have access to the same fundamental assumptions; in this category every utterance is pressed into service to affirm the social order. Speech in this case exercises a solidarity-maintaining function closely comparable to religion as Durkheim saw it functioning in primitive society. The second category of speech distinguished by Bernstein is employed in social situations where the speakers do not accept or necessarily know one another's fundamental assumptions. Speech has then the primary function of making explicit unique individual perceptions, and bridging different initial assumptions. The two categories of speech arise in social systems which correspond to those which Durkheim indicated as governed by mechanical and organic solidarity. So Bernstein would deserve the attention of anthropologists if only because he is sympathetic to a Durkheimian sociology of knowledge, one which was originally worked out by comparing ritual as a medium of communication in tribal and in industrial society. He says that:

different speech systems or codes create for their speakers different orders of relevance and relation. The experience of the speakers may then be transformed by what is made significant or relevant by different speech systems. As the child learns his speech, or, in the terms I shall use here, learns specific codes which regulate his verbal acts, he learns the requirements of his social structure. The experience of the child is transformed by the learning generated by his own, apparently voluntary acts of speech. The social structure becomes in this way the substratum of the child's experience essentially through the manifold consequence of the linguistic process. From this point of view, every time the child speaks or listens, the social structure is reinforced in him and his social identity shaped. (From his paper entitled *A Sociolinguistic Approach to Socialisation*, 1970)

He distinguishes two different types of linguistic codes. One he calls the elaborated code, in which, as he says, the speaker selects from a wide range of syntactic alternatives, which are flexibly organized; this speech requires complex planning. In the other, which he calls the restricted code, the speaker draws from a much narrower range of syntactic alternatives, and these alternatives are more rigidly organized. The elaborated code is adapted to enable a speaker to make his own intentions explicit, to elucidate general principles. Each type of speech code is generated in its own type of social matrix. As I understand it, the differences between the two coding systems depend entirely on the relation of each to the social context. The restricted code is deeply enmeshed in the immediate social structure, utterances have a double purpose: they convey information, yes, but they also express the social structure, embellish and reinforce it. The second function is the dominant one, whereas the elaborated code emerges as a form of speech which is progressively more and more free of the second function. Its primary function is to organize thought processes, distinguish and combine ideas. In its more extreme, elaborate form it is so much disengaged from the normal social structure that it may even come to dominate the latter and require the social group to be structured around the speech, as in the case of a university lecture.

It is essential to realize that the elaborated code is a product of the division of labour. The more highly differentiated the social system, the more specialized the decision-making roles – then the more the pressure for explicit channels of communication concerning a wide range of policies and their consequences. The demands of the industrial system are pressing hard now upon education to produce more and more verbally articulate people who will be promoted to entrepreneurial roles. By inference, the restricted code will be found where these pressures are weakest. Professor Bernstein's research in London schools and families finds that the codes are instilled into children from their earliest infancy by their mothers. Each speech system is developed in its corresponding system of family control. He asks mothers of working-class and middle-class families how they control their children under five; what happens if the child won't go to bed? won't eat? breaks the crockery? From their detailed responses he constructs a distinctive pattern of values, a distinctive concept of the person and of morality.

Let me describe the two kinds of family role system. Restricted codes are generated in what he calls the positional family. The child in this family is controlled by the continual building-up of a sense of social pattern: of ascribed role categories. If he asks 'Why must I do this?' the answer is in terms of relative position. Because I said so (hierarchy). Because you're a boy (sex role). Because children always do (age status). Because you're the oldest (seniority). As he grows, his experience flows into a grid of role categories; right and wrong are learnt in terms of the given structure; he himself is seen only in relation to that structure. The child's curiosity in working-class or some aristocratic families is harnessed to the task of sustaining his social environment. Let me quote briefly from Bernstein himself. Differences in speech are taken to be

indices of a particular form of communication; they are not in any sense accidental but are contingent on a form of social structure. These differences I shall argue indicate the use of a linguistic code. It is a (restricted) code which does not facilitate the verbal elaboration of meaning; it is a code which sensitizes the user to a particular form of social relationship which is unambiguous, where the authority is clear-cut and serves as a guide to action. It is a code which helps to sustain solidarity with the group at the cost of verbal signalling of the unique difference of its members. It is a code which facilitates the ready transformation of feeling into action. It is a code where changes in meaning are more likely to be signalled non-verbally than through changes in verbal selections ... How does this way of translating experience come about? What in the culture is responsible for the speech system?... Different social structures will generate different speech systems. These speech systems or codes entail for the individual specific principles of choice which regulate the selections he makes from language at both the syntactic and lexical level. What the individual actually says, from a developmental perspective, transforms him in the act of saying.

As the child learns his speech or in our terms learns specific codes which regulate his verbal acts he learns the requirements of his social structure. From this point of view every time the child speaks the social structure of which he is a part is reinforced in him, and his social identity develops and is constrained. The social structure becomes for the developing child his psychological reality by the shaping of his acts of speech. If this is the case, then the processes which orient the child to his world and the kind of relationships he imposes are triggered off initially and systematically reinforced by the implications of the speech system. Underlying the general pattern of the child's speech are initial sets of choices, in-built preferences for some alternatives rather than others, planning processes which develop and are stabilized through time – coding principles through which orientation is given to social, intellectual and emotional referents. (1964: 56–7)

When a child learns a restricted code he learns to perceive language in a particular way. Language is not perceived as a set of theoretical possibilities which can be transferred into a facility for the communication of unique experience. Speech is not primarily a means for a voyage from one self to the other. In as much as this is so then areas of the self are not likely to be differentiated by speech and so become the object of special perceptual activity. It is also likely that the motivations of others will not serve as starting points for inquiry and verbal elaboration. Of some importance, the identity of the individual will be refracted to him by the concrete symbols of his group rather than creating a problem to be solved by his own unique investigations ... A critical aspect of the family is the means of expression of authority, particularly the type of verbal interaction authority relationships create. I shall argue that associated with parents limited to a restricted code is a specific form of authority relation. Authority can be expressed so as to limit the chances of verbal interaction with the relationship, or authority can be expressed so as to increase verbal interaction. The area of discretion available to the child may be reduced to an uncompromising acceptance, withdrawal or rebellion within the authority relationship, or the social context of control may permit a number of responses on the part of the child ... If the appeals are status-oriented then the behaviour of the child is referred to some general or local rule which constrains conduct, 'shouldn't you clean your teeth', you 'don't behave yourself like that on a bus', 'children in grammar schools are expected to behave rather differently'. Status appeals may also relate the child's behaviour to the rules which regulate his conduct with reference to age, sex or age relationships, e.g. 'Little boys don't play with dolls', 'you should be able to stop doing that by now', 'you don't talk to your father, teacher, social worker, etc., like that'. These are important implications of status appeals. If they are not obeyed the relationship can quickly change to reveal naked power and may become punitive. Status appeals are impersonal. They rely for their effectiveness upon the status of the regulator. The effect of these appeals is to transmit the culture or local culture in such a way as to increase the similarity of the regulated with others of his group. If the child rebels he is challenging very quickly the culture of which he is a part, and it is this which tends to force the regulator into taking punitive action. (1964:59–60)

By contrast, in the family system which Professor Bernstein calls personal a fixed pattern of roles is not celebrated, but rather the autonomy and unique value of the individual. When the child asks a question the mother feels bound to answer it by as full an explanation as she knows. The curiosity of the child is used to increase his verbal control, to elucidate causal relations, to teach him to assess the consequences of his acts. Above all his behaviour is controlled by being made sensitive to the personal feelings of others, by inspecting his own feelings. Why can't I do it? Because your father's feeling worried; because I've got a headache. How would you like it if you were a fly? or a dog? The child tends to be controlled by person-oriented appeals:

In these appeals the conduct of the child is related to the feelings of the regulator (parent) or the significance of the act, its meaning is related explicitly to the regulated, to the child, e.g. 'Daddy will be pleased, hurt, disappointed, angry, ecstatic if you go on doing this'. 'If you go on doing this you will be miserable when the cat has a nasty pain' ... Control is effected through either the verbal manipulation of feelings and through the establishment of reasons which link the child to his acts. In this way the child has access to the regulator as a person and he has access to the significance of his own acts as they relate to him as consequences . . . The status-oriented appeals rely for their effectiveness upon differences in status whereas the person-oriented appeals rely more upon the manipulation of thought and feeling. (Bernstein, 1964: 60)

In this way the child is freed from a system of rigid positions, but made a prisoner of a system of feelings and abstract principles. The personal system of family control is well adapted to develop verbal skills: the child will do better in school examinations as a result of his control of the elaborated code. He may shoot forward to the top of the wider society, become Prime Minister, Head of UNO; the sky's the limit. Underlying this family system is anxiety about the child's development and educational success. It is probably not inspired by ambition. More likely it is inspired by the knowledge that in a changing world the only ticket anyone can hold for staying in a privileged niche is education. The child is being educated for a changing social environment. As his parents move from one town or country to another in response to the need for professional mobility, the child grows in a family system which is relatively unstructured, a collection of unique feelings and needs. Right and wrong are learnt in terms of his response to those feelings. Instead of internalizing any particular social structure, his inside is continually stirred into a ferment of ethical sensibilities. We can immediately and from our own experience recognize this as the basis for the move from ritual to ethics. There is no need to indicate the clichés from the literary and philosophical output of the last 100 years which validate the system.

To sum up Basil Bernstein's approach in a diagram: one line expresses the way that patterns of family control are progressively detached from the immediate social structure of the family and local community and progressively co-ordinated with the demands of the wider industrial social structure (Bernstein, 1970).

Diagram 1: Family Control

Control

Positional → Personal

The other line studies the effect of the same industrial pressures upon speech. Verbal communication is progressively detached from its service to the immediate social context and elaborated for its use in the widest social structures of all.

Diagram 2: Speech Codes

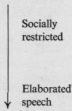

Socially
restricted

Elaborated
speech

In the process, note that as speech sheds its social harness, it becomes a very specialized, independent tool of thought. Basil Bernstein has plausibly suggested that the emancipation of speech from social control underlies some variations in religious worship. The following table is the result of our discussions together. It is very impressionistic and designed more than anything to help follow in imagination the kind of transitions that can be studied in this framework.

Admittedly, there are several difficulties about this table. To understand it we should look first at A and B. A represents most primitive cultures in which speech forms are firmly embedded in a stable social structure. The primary use of language is to affirm and embellish the social structure which rests upon unchallengeable metaphysical assumptions. In such a system we would expect to find that the admired virtues are those which unquestioningly uphold the social structure, and the hated sins are transgressions against it. Since individual motivation is irrele-

Diagram 3: General Cosmological Ideas

(i) cardinal virtues
(ii) cardinal sins
(iii) the idea of the self
(iv) art form

Speech
Socially restricted

A   C

A	C
(i) piety, honour (respect for roles)	(i) sincerity, authenticity
(ii) formal transgressions against social structure	(ii) sins against the self, hypocrisy, cruelty, acceptance of frustration
(iii) self, passive, undifferentiated element in a structured environment	(iii) internally differentiated agent, attempting to control unstructured environment
(iv) primitive: structural elaborations upon social categories, humans as cardboard allegorical figures	(iv) romantic: triumph of individual over structure (escape, brief happiness, etc.)

Family Control System

Positional   *Personal*

Positional	Personal
(i) truth, duty	(i) personal success, doing good to humanity
(ii) cardinal sin is failure to respond to demands of social structure	(ii) generalized guilt, individual and collective
(iii) active agent, internally differentiated, responding to roles	(iii) subject alone
(iv) classical: triumph of structure over individual	(iv) professionalism: overriding concern with techniques and materials of creative process

B   D

Speech elaborated

vant to the demand for performance, we would expect to find little reflection on the notion of the self; the individual is hardly concerned as a complex agent. On the contrary, the self is seen as a passive arena in which external forces play out their conflicts. This would be the social structure to give rise to totemic thought systems and to art forms which celebrate social dichotomies and confrontations. In these the relation of the individual to society is hardly considered. This general class emerges as appropriate wherever literacy is low and the social structure stable.

In square B, speech and thought have been elaborated as specialized tools for decision-making, but the social structure still retains a strong grip on its members, even to the extent that its underlying assumptions are not challenged. Elaborated speech in this case is still in the service of the social structure, but uses the philosophical reflections at which it has become adept for examining and justifying those assumptions. This would be the square for Aristotle. The result of this reflection of speech and thought on the social structure would be an awareness of the demands of the latter upon the individual and of the possibility of the individual not responding adequately. Truth and duty would be the primary virtues. They express the confidence that the social structure rests upon a rational foundation which justifies its claim to allegiance. As a result of the capacity for reflection and as an expression of the new independence of thought, we would expect the self to be accorded a much more active role. The danger of the individual rejecting the claims of society would here be recognized, though condemned. Does it help to suggest that classical drama, Oedipus and le Cid, depicts these attitudes?

In squares C and D the social structure has lost its grip. Square C, according to Bernstein, is unstable, a transitional phase. For example a mother belonging to the professional classes by her own education and aspirations, married into a working-class environment, might bring up her children by the techniques of personal control, but through the rest of their social relations they would be obliged to use speech of the restricted code. Here the individual is valued above the social structure; hence the literature of revolt, Rimbaud, or D. H. Lawrence.

In so far as there is a literature for this square, we have to assume that individuals reared in it have made in their lifetime the move from C to D, have become verbally articulate in elaborated codes.

We can understand square D most easily, for it includes ourselves. I cannot go further without trying to be more specific about who, in our contemporary society, fits into squares B and D. What is the distribution of people using elaborated speech codes between positional and personal family control systems? Start with square B. The positional family develops on the assumption that roles should be defined clearly and the elaboration of speech, in so far as it is used to sustain role patterns, reduces ambiguity. Here we would expect to find aristocracies whose aspirations are relatively fixed and whose role structure is clearly ascribed. Also certain sections of the middle class will be here. The military profession, for example, demands unambiguous allocation of roles; the legal profession lives by reducing role ambiguity. There are other highly educated sectors of modern society whose profession encourages them to favour positional control systems. The work of engineers, concerned primarily with abstract relations between material objects, does not lead them to use the elaborated code to reflect critically on the nature of social relations. That they should tend towards positional family systems becomes clearer when we see how the other square, D, is filled. Here are the people who live by using elaborated speech to review and revise existing categories of thought. To challenge received ideas is their very bread and butter. They (or should I say we?) practise a professional detachment towards any given pattern of experience. The more boldly and comprehensively they apply their minds to rethinking, the better their chances of professional success. Thus the value of their radical habit of thought is socially confirmed, and reinforced. For with the rise to professional eminence comes the geographical and social mobility that detaches them from their original community. With such validation, they are likely to raise their children in the habit of intellectual challenge and not to impose a positional control pattern. How much more likely are they to prefer personal forms of control if the area of their professional thinking deals with human relations: psychologists, anthropologists, novelists, philosophers, political scientists. The professions which deal with the expression of personal feelings rather than with abstract principles are also found here. This is the square in which ideas about morality and the self get detached from the social structure. This would be the niche in which to consider Existentialism and the deep pre-occupation of our day with the technical process of artistic creation.

The positional child, who knows the pattern in which he belongs, cannot understand the anguish which Sartre has described so poignantly in *Words*, the biography of his first ten years of life (1964). In the home of his domineering and histrionic grandfather he and his widowed mother were appendages, serving mainly to provide the grandparents with emotional satisfaction. From infancy he was tormented with the consciousness that his existence had no justification. There was no society organized in general categories of age, sex and hierarchy in which his developing role could be seen as necessary to some overall pattern. Only the promise of personal success, the renown of future genius, could justify his life in the patternless adult world which made such unconvincing pretence of valuing him for his loveable personality. This dominant anxiety of childhood is clearly related to his later philosophical position. Bernstein suggests that problems of self-justification arise in the personal family – and was not the Reformation about self-justification?

Some may argue that Bernstein's contrast of positional with personal family is no different from the old distinction between achieved and ascribed status. This is an error. The positional/personal contrast rides at a higher level of abstraction. In the personal family, true enough, all roles have to be achieved, but the converse does not hold good. In some positional families, within the ascribed framework, important roles have to be achieved. For example in military families there is a strong emphasis on achievement. The contrast of achieved/acquired status needs to take account of the different realms of achievement.

For reasons which may now be clear, it is easier for us (writers and readers) to recognize and sympathize with the aspirations of one raised in a personal family than with the person raised in the positional family. Certainly I believe that the Bog Irish have suffered from such a blank in the imaginative sympathy of their pastors, whose personal outlook conforms to their special niche in the professional ladder. The latter might take a more generous view of tenacious ritualism if they saw the impoverished power of response to condensed symbols of all kinds which lies in the direction they are leading and if they could value ritualistic forms of commitment as such. It must be difficult for the child reared on abstract principles in the personal family to draw moral lines, to be bound by promises – for unquestioned boundaries have never been part of his upbringing. The child in the positional family grows into a set of unchallenged categories, which are expressed by non-verbal symbols as well as by words.

Bernstein's work on the social structuring of speech in London families challenges the anthropologist in many, very difficult fields. At first sight all ritual would seem to be a form of restricted code. It is a form of verbal utterance whose meanings are largely implicit; many of them are carried along standardized non-verbal channels. Indeed, since Malinowski no one has thought to interpret the language of magic apart from the symbolic actions and apart from the whole social context. Ritual is generally highly coded. Its units are organized to standard types in advance of use. Lexically its meanings are local and particular. Syntactically it is available to all members of the community. The syntax is rigid, it offers a small range of alternative forms. Indeed so limited does the syntactic range tend to be that many anthropologists find that a simple binary analysis is sufficient to elucidate the meanings of myth or ritual symbols. Bernstein himself has suggested that his definitions should be applicable to other symbolic forms – he has suggested music (1965: 166). He has also recognized that in any one case elaboration and restriction will be relative. Obviously there are technical difficulties in applying this comparison of speech and ritual forms. However, at first glance we seem to have a ready-made solution to our opening question. The causes of anti-ritualism today in middle-class European and American communities would appear to be a predictable result of a process of socialization in which the child never internalizes a pattern of social statuses and never experiences authoritative control which exalts the self-evident property of a social system to command obedience. Symbols of solidarity and hierarchy have not been part of his education. Consequently a form of aesthetic experience is closed to him. As Bernstein emphasizes:

> It is important to realize that a restricted code carries its own aesthetic. It will tend to develop a metaphoric range of considerable power, a simplicity and directness, a vitality and rhythm; it should not be disvalued. Psychologically, it unites the speaker to his kin and to his local community. (1965: 165)

It is tempting to equate the restricted code with ritualism and to leave the matter there. In many anthropologists' accounts of a pastoral or hunting economy there appears the outline of an ox or wild pig or antelope quartered and subdivided, with a legend indicating the category of kin to which each segment is allocated. Such a chart showing the correct distribution of game or of sacrificial meat summarizes the main social categories. Similarly the first fruits celebrations of agriculturalists. Each feast reaffirms the categories visibly and publicly. Primitive rules of purity also support the social categories and give them external, physical reality. Clearly the words which accompany these distributions carry a small part only of the significance of the occasion. The comparable situations in family life would be the spatial layout of chairs in the living room which convey the hierarchy of rank and sex, the celebration of Sunday dinner, and for some families, presumably those in which a restricted code is used, every meal and every rising, bathing and bed-time is structured to express and support the social order. Bernstein's fully personal family, then, would be one in which no meals were taken in common and no hierarchy recognized, but in which the mother would attempt to meet the unique needs of each child by creating an entirely individual environment of time-table and services around each one of her brood; early supper for this one to go to choir practice, late supper for that one coming back from an excursion, hospitality for that other one's friends and so on; food selections too would be on an individual basis. How could such a child ever learn to respond to a communally exerted authority? His ears would not be attuned to catch the unspoken messages of a restricted code. Hence some of the deafness and antipathy to ritualism in our day.

This would be fine and an end of the argument if, as was commonly held, all primitive peoples were ritualist and if the movement away from magicality were indeed able to be plotted along a graph showing more and more the effects of the division of labour on family behaviour. But I have mentioned already the unritualistic pygmies; then there are the Basseri who have so little that can be called religion, the Anuak who are much more interested in counteracting witchcraft than in worshipping God or indulging in metaphysical speculations, and probably a host more of so-called primitive tribes who share with the most industrially advanced nations a lack of interest in ritual. We shall need to look closely at the social structures of these tribes, to find a set of variables which will be consistent both with the Bernstein effect among ourselves and with what is known about primitive social structure and cosmology. This exercise will take us a long way from Bernstein's analysis, but I intend to return to it at the end. No doubt readers are more interested in themselves than in exotic tribesmen and I regret that I am not able to develop more fully the parallel between the positional home and the primitive ritualist. Let me at least include some suggestions thrown out by Bernstein (in a personal communication) on the types of religious behaviour he would expect to be associated with types of family control. The primitive ritualist, in his ascribed social system, expresses cosmic orientations and moral directives in condensed symbols. The home which is organized around positional values has comparable methods of explanation and control. In a community composed of such homes God would be also known through the restricted code. Theological concepts about him would not be fully elucidated, he would be known by his attributes as manifested in the social structure. Knowing God would be subject to the same restrictions as knowing the mother: the code of speech would not provide means for reflecting upon or inspecting the relationship verbally. The religious cult would be expected to correspond in style to the family rituals and therefore to be fixed and ritualistic. Similarly the definition of sin would be more concerned with specific external actions than with internal motivation.

In diagram 3 the idea of the self was progressively detached from the social structure. So, as ritualism declines, the idea of God becomes more intimate. But as God comes nearer he is diminished in glory and power. This hypothesis can be recognized as thoroughly Durkheimian. For the cosmology, based on its particular hierarchy of values and upholding a particular pattern of behaviour, is derived from society. As the grip of his immediate society on the individual tightens or slackens something happens to his religious attitudes.

There is an awkward paradox in this presentation. For as a Londoner gets drawn more and more into the vortex of industrial society his religious ideas seem to approximate more and more to those of the pygmy. He believes in spontaneity, friendship, freedom, and goodness of heart: he rejects formality, magic, doctrinal logic-chopping and condemnation of his fellow humans for their wrong-doings. This paradox is due to a distortion in the comparison caused by the effects of the division of labour. Pygmies cannot be equated with preachers, journalists and dons. The argument will have to go a long way before we can pick up this paradox and resolve it. In the meanwhile, note what the Bernstein effect amounts to. As a result of definable pressures on home and school there is an increasing tendency to rear children by personal, elaborated speech code methods. This produces a child acutely sensitive to the feelings of others, and interested in his own internal states. It follows that such an education will predispose a person to ethical preoccupations, for while it opens up his vocabulary of feeling it also denies him any sense of pattern in his social life. He must therefore look for some justification of his existence outside the performance of set rules. He can only find it in good works on behalf of humanity in general or in personal success, or both. Hence the drive towards a purely ethical religion.

3   The Bog Irish

The Bog Irishman in his faithfulness to the rule of Friday abstinence is undeniably like the primitive ritualist. Magical rules
have always an expressive function. Whatever other functions
they perform, disciplinary, anxiety-reducing, or sanctioning of
moral codes, they have first and foremost a symbolic function.
The official symbolism of Friday abstinence was originally personal mortification, a small weekly celebration of the annual
celebration of Good Friday. Thus it pointed directly to Calvary
and Redemption. It could hardly have a more central load of
meaning for Christian worship. In reporting that it has become
empty and meaningless, what is meant is that its symbols are
no longer seen to point in that direction or anywhere in particular.

Yet symbols which are tenaciously adhered to can hardly be
dismissed as altogether meaningless. They must mean something.
We can start by asking what are the most poignant experiences
of the Irish girl who has left her home to do service in London
hotels or hospitals, or of the Irish man who arrives looking for
big, quick money in construction work. If they have friends and
kin to find them lodgings, their sense of exile is softened by a
sense of continuity, the Irish newspapers sold outside Church
after Mass, the weekly dances in the parish hall. There is a sense
of belonging. If no such welcome is arranged, they are likely to
see on the doors of lodging houses: 'No Irish, no coloured'. Then
the sense of exile and of boundary is sharper. This is what the
rule of Friday abstinence can signify. No empty symbol, it means
allegiance to a humble home in Ireland and to a glorious tradition

in Rome. These allegiances are something to be proud of in the humiliations of the unskilled labourer's lot. At its lowest it means what haggis and the pipes mean to Scots abroad on Burns' night. At its most it means what abstaining from pork meant to the venerable Eleazar as narrated in 2 Maccabees.

The Catholic hierarchy in England today are under pressure to underestimate the expressive function of ritual. Catholics are exhorted to invent individual acts of almsgiving as a more meaningful celebration of Friday. But why Friday? Why celebrate at all? Why not be good and generous all the time? As soon as symbolic action is denied value in its own right, the flood-gates of confusion are opened. Symbols are the only means of communication. They are the only means of expressing value; the main instruments of thought, the only regulators of experience. For any communication to take place, the symbols must be structured. For communication about religion to take place, the structure of the symbols must be able to express something relevant to the social order. If a people takes a symbol that originally meant one thing, and twists it to mean something else, and energetically holds on to that subverted symbol, its meanings for their personal life must be very profound. Who would dare to despise the cult of Friday abstinence who has not himself endured the life of the Irish labourer in London?

Friday abstinence must be interpreted under the same rubric as Jewish abstinence from pork. In *Purity and Danger* I argued that the dietary rules in Leviticus xi afford a shorthand summary of the categories of Israelite culture. The pig is not singled out for special abhorrence more than the camel and the rock badger. The dietary rules, I suggested, should be taken as a whole and related to the totality of symbolic structures organizing the universe. In this way the abominations are seen as anomalies within a particular logical scheme (Douglas, 1966: ch. 3). Since writing this, useful criticisms have been made. Dr S. Strizower (1966) has pointed out that I overlooked the importance of restrictive dietary rules in setting the Israelites apart from other people and in expressing their sense of apartness. Ralph Bulmer has argued that if my interpretation of the whole set of rules as carrying a condensed classification of the universe be conceded, it still does not explain the particular abhorrence of the flesh of the pig (1967: 21). Why should this one animal be singled out to be the chief representative and vanguard of all other abominations? The answer to both would seem to be in the two books of Maccabees. This is the narrative of how Judas Maccabeus led the people of Israel against their conquerors, the Greeks.

1 Maccabees i, 21. And after Antiochus had ravaged Egypt in the 143rd year, he returned and sent up against Israel ... 23. And he proudly entered into the sanctuary and took away the golden altar ... 26. ... and there was great mourning in Israel ... 29. And all the house of Jacob was covered with confusion. 32–8. He attacked and destroyed the city, threw down the walls, took the women captive ... and built the city of David with a great and strong wall and with strong towers and made it a fortress for them ... 39. ... and defiled the holy place ... 40. And the inhabitants of Jerusalem fled away by reason of them, and the city was made a habitation of strangers; and she became a stranger to her own seed and her children forsook her.

Not content with political and military victory, King Antiochus ordered all the nations under him to leave their own laws.

45 ... And many of Israel consented to his service: and they sacrificed to idols and profaned the Sabbath.

Throughout the subsequent narrative of the overthrow of the invading armies and the purification of the temple three themes are treated as co-ordinate symbols:

defilement of the temple
defilement of the body
breach of the law.

The temple is finally rebuilt and rededicated, with high walls and strong towers round about (1 Maccabees iv, 60); a necessary military precaution. But the leaders of Israel also took as drastic precautions against the defilement of their bodies (2 Maccabees v, 27):

But Judas Maccabeus ... had withdrawn himself into a desert place, and there lived among the wild beasts in the mountains with his company: and they continued feeding on herbs, that they might not be partakers of the pollution.

Those who circumcised or observed the Sabbath in secret were brutally killed by the conquerors. It is clear here that any of the rules, dietary and other, and any among the dietary rules, were equally held sacred and their breach equally held polluting. But Antiochus ordered swine to be immolated on their altars (1 Maccabees i, 50) and took eating of swine's flesh as a symbol of submission (2 Maccabees vi). So it was he, by this action, who forced into prominence the rule concerning pork as the critical symbol of group allegiance. Circumcision, after all, is a private matter concerning the private parts of a person. Observing the Sabbath, also, does not necessarily impinge on other people's lives or at least only periodically. Refusal of commensality is a more total rejection of social intercourse. If the heathen eat pork, the pork-avoiding Israelite cannot join their meals. In a greatly lessened degree, if a Catholic is invited out to dine on Friday, his ritual allegiance may be an affront to his hosts, only because it is not one they share. Thus pork avoidance and Friday abstinence gain significance as symbols of allegiance simply by their lack of meaning for other cultures. The splendid passage describing Eleazar's trial explains how eating pork came to be abhorred as an act of betrayal as well as of defilement.

2 Maccabees vi, 18. Eleazar, one of the chief of the scribes, a man advanced in years and of a comely countenance, was pressed to open his mouth to eat swine's flesh. 19. But he, choosing rather a most glorious death than a hateful life, went forward voluntarily to the torment . . . 21. But they that stood by, being moved with wicked pity, for the old friendship they had with the man, taking him aside, desired that flesh might be brought which it was lawful for him to eat, that he might make as if he had eaten, as the king had commanded, of the flesh of the sacrifice. 22. That by so doing he might be delivered from death. And for the sake of their old friendship with the man they did him this courtesy. 23. But he began to consider the dignity of his age and his ancient years and the inbred honour of his grey head and his good life and conversation from a child: and he answered without delay, according to the ordinances of the holy law made by God, saying that

he would rather be sent into the other world. 24. For it doth not become our age, said he, to dissemble: whereby many young persons might think that Eleazar, at the age of fourscore and ten years, was gone over to the life of the heathens: 25. And so, they, through my dissimulation and for a little time of a corruptible life should be deceived, and hereby I should bring a stain and a curse upon my old age . . . 27. Wherefore, by departing manfully out of this life, I shall shew myself worthy of my old age. 28. And I shall leave an example of fortitude to young men, if with a ready mind and constancy I suffer an honourable death, for the most venerable and most holy laws. And having spoken thus, he was forthwith carried to execution.

Notice that it is not one law, but all the laws for which he dies, and that the execrable character of pig itself as an animal or form of food does not enter into the discussion. Nor does it enter into the next chapter in which seven brothers and their mother were apprehended and compelled by the King to eat swine's flesh. In all the gruesome description of how their tongues were cut out, their heads scalped and their bodies fried alive to the merriment of pagan onlookers in huge frying pans, nothing is said whatever about the abominable character of pig. But after such historic acts of heroism, no wonder the avoidance of pork became a specially powerful symbol of allegiance for the Jewish people and so attracted the later hellenizing exegesis that looked to the moral attributes of the pig. Whereas this symbol in origin owed its meaning only to its place in a total pattern of symbols, for which it came to stand, as a result of its prominence in persecution. We belong to a generation whose perception of symbols is blurred except in familiar social contexts. So it may be easier to sympathize with the irritation of the cook in *King Solomon's Mines* at the unswerving obedience of the Zulu, Umslopogas, to his dietary laws. If two symbolic systems are confronted, they begin to form, even by their opposition, a single whole. In this totality each half may be represented to the other by a single element which is made to jump out of context to perform this role. Other people select among our external symbols of allegiance those which offend or amuse them most. So Shifra Strizower is right. Further account of the apartness of the people of Israel and of their beleaguered history would have given more meaning to their dietary laws. The story of Maccabees teaches that the Israelites took the purity of the temple and the purity of the human body to represent adherence to all the details of the law and so a total turning of each person in his own body and of the whole nation in the temple and in the law towards God. For when they cleansed and rebuilt the temple (1 Maccabees iv, 42) 'he chose priests without blemish whose will was set upon the law of God'. The high walls they built around Mount Sion and the strong guard they set upon their mouths were the symbolic ramparts of their commitment to their religion.

Perhaps it is true that Friday abstinence became a wall behind which the Catholics in England retired too smugly. But it was the only ritual which brought Christian symbols down into the kitchen and larder and on to the dinner table in the manner of Jewish rules of impurity. To take away one symbol that meant something is no guarantee that the spirit of charity will flow in its place. It might have been safer to build upon that small symbolic wall in the hope that eventually it could come to surround Mount Sion. But we have seen that those who are responsible for ecclesiastical decisions are only too likely to have been made, by the manner of their education, insensitive to non-verbal signals and dull to their meaning. This is central to the difficulties of Christianity today. It is as if the liturgical signal boxes were manned by colour-blind signalmen.

I will now give some space to the question of Friday abstinence to demonstrate that there is indeed a clear movement in educated Catholic circles in England, a move from symbolic to ethical action. But it is a less important example than my second one, the change in the attitude to the Eucharist. Friday abstinence was never anything more than a disciplinary rule. No special sacramental efficacy was officially imputed to the act, negatively or positively, whereas the doctrine of the Eucharist is as magically sacramental as any tribal religion.

Some anthropologists reading this may be as confused as to the nature of Friday abstinence from meat as the most benighted of the faithful. They may even share Goodenough's belief that the focus of the ritual is not on penitence, but on a positive celebration of fish as against meat. He has argued ingeniously (1956: 50f.) that fish, which Catholic housewives queue for on Fridays, is a powerful condensed symbol of Christ and that herein lies the true explanation of the observance. However there is no rule about eating fish; only a rule about abstaining from flesh meat. In February 1966 Pope Paul VI issued a decree on fasting and abstinence. He expounded the tradition of penitence, 'a religious and personal act which has as its aim love and surrender to God'. Citing numerous Old Testament instances of the fast as pleasing to God, and citing Christ's example in the New Testament, he describes acts of penance as 'participating in a special way in the infinite expiation of Christ ... Thus the task of bearing in his body and soul the death of our Lord affects the whole life of the baptized person at every instant and in every aspect.' He goes on to condemn any form of penitence which is 'purely external'. Recognizing that very different conditions prevail in rich and poor countries, he proceeds to revise the Church laws on fasting and abstinence, concentrating them in the season of Lent and otherwise requiring abstinence only on Fridays. These minimal penitential days and seasons are intended to 'unite the faithful in a common celebration of penitence'. At the same time he invites the Bishops to substitute wholly or in part other penitential exercises (*Paenitemine*, 17 February 1966).

An article in *L'Osservatore Romano* (20 February 1966) by W. Bertrams (a canon lawyer at the Gregorian University) comments on the decree and gives it a little extra twist away from ritual and towards ethics and social justice:

Indeed, the faithful must be taught that the Christian spirit of penitence demands also the voluntary privation of things which are not absolutely necessary, so that the money which would have been spent in obtaining them may be used instead for works of charity.

A year later the English hierarchy takes up the invitation to adapt the penitential legislation to local conditions. A letter is issued from the Archbishop's house (21 July 1967) seeking the views of all clergy and laity. The letter shows no sense of history or of the value of symbolic action; moreover it shows a strange ambivalence to the subject in hand. It starts firmly by announcing that there is no question of simply abolishing Friday abstinence, but of asking whether an obligatory rule of Friday abstinence achieves its purpose today. What the purpose is, the letter treats very summarily, and goes on with:

Some consider that the obligation should be abolished and instead Fridays should be marked by prayer, voluntary abstinence or other penitential exercises. It is argued that obligatory Friday abstinence is not necessarily a penance and that modern conditions make it difficult to observe it. For the most part, professional and working people have their midday meal away from home, often in a canteen. Again, social events are often fixed for a Friday. And whilst an alternative dish is often available, it is questioned whether it is advisable in our mixed society for a Catholic to appear singular in this matter. Non-Catholics know and accept that we do not eat meat on Fridays but often they do not understand why we do not, and in consequence regard us as odd.

Echoes of the Reformed Synagogue! Arguing that it is not a hardship to avoid meat, and then adding that there is too much hardship for those eating away from home and social embarrassment for those dining out, this seems an inadequate statement to use for consulting the mind of the faithful. When the consultation was concluded, the following was issued:

As respect for the moral law decreases, the need for self-denial grows greater. Many Catholics have begun to ask themselves if going without meat on Friday is penance enough. Some find it no penance at all. Meanwhile, in Asia, Africa and South America many Catholics have to go without meat not only on Friday but every day. Millions are starving or at least underfed.

The Bishops have therefore decided that the best way of carrying out our Lord's command to do penance is for each of us to choose our own way of self-denial each Friday . . . (31 December 1967)

Thus was the old ritual abolished. In the old days the child admonished to eat his tapioca for the sake of starving millions would be puzzled to know how this obedience would benefit the hungry. The problem of how to benefit the hungry by not abstaining from meat does not arise. The Catholic Institute for International Relations quickly produced a collecting box marked 'Friday fund. One meal a day', and sent it around with an appeal: 'Friday Apathy or Friday Action: Will you put a little away for others each Friday? Boxes from C I I R'. Now there is no cause for others to 'regard us as odd'. Friday no longer rings the great cosmic symbols of expiation and atonement: it is not symbolic at all, but a practical day for the organization of charity. Now the English Catholics are like everyone else.

Interestingly, the American bishops did much better (from the ritualist, anthropological point of view) than the English in their handling of the same opportunity. There is no down-grading of the symbolic function, more sense of history, more recognition of the need for symbolic solidarity with the past and present body of the Church. Their pastoral statement begins with admirable directness:

Christ died for us on Friday. Gratefully remembering this, Catholic peoples from time immemorial have set apart Friday for special penitential observance by which they gladly suffer with Christ, that they may one day be glorified with him. This is the heart of the tradition of abstinence from meat on Fridays ... Changing circumstances, including economic, dietary and social elements, have made some of our people feel that the renunciation of the eating of meat is not always and for everyone the most effective means of practising penance.

Their sense of liturgical continuity comes out in a list of recommendations which start by saying 'Friday should be in each week something of what Lent is in the entire year. For this reason we urge all to prepare for that weekly Easter by freely making of every Friday a day of mortification in prayerful remembrance of the passion of Jesus Christ.' Thus the liturgical year is encapsulated in the liturgical week. They go on specially to commend voluntary abstinence from flesh meat as a means of observing Friday:

(*a*) We shall thus freely and out of love of Christ crucified show our solidarity with the generation of believers to whom this practice frequently became, especially in time of persecution and of great poverty, no mean evidence of fidelity to Christ and His Church.

(*b*) We shall thus also remind ourselves that as Christians, although immersed in the world and sharing its life, we must preserve a saving and necessary difference from the spirit of the world. Our deliberate personal abstinence from meat, more especially because no longer required by law, will be an outward sign of inward spiritual values that we cherish. (Pastoral statement of Conference of Catholic Bishops on Penitential Observance, Washington, D.C., 18 November 1966)

It is easy to recognize in the banality of the English hierarchy's attitude the working of the Bernstein effect, surely not among all the Bishops, but certainly among their advisors. It is puzzling to know how the American hierarchy came to take a different view of symbolic action. It is unlikely that their secretariats are not equally staffed by new men, reared in personal homes and masters of the elaborated code. It may be that the greater sociological awareness of the Americans makes the difference. For the sociologist of religion would be superficial indeed if he were not aware of the power of symbols to order experience. No one would deny value in its own right to the symbolic function who takes time and perspective to reflect objectively on the issue. Those who belittle it are responding shortsightedly to their own subjective situation in home and in society.

I seem to have taken a very heavy hammer to crack a small liturgical nut. Friday abstinence is a disciplinary rule, a mere detail. Although this book is not intended primarily for anthropologists, I have written about this theme at length for their interest. For anthropologists often exhort one another to turn to contemporary religions for their material and particularly to Christianity. Dietary restrictions are deep in their traditional subject matter and I wish to show that modern examples are as susceptible to the modes of analysis we employ as are primitive ones. Why not? The only difficulty hitherto has been the lack of a frame of analysis for comparing ourselves and tribal societies along the series from high magicality to low. In the 1960s Bernstein's work on ourselves and Turnbull's work on the pygmies enables this framework to be set up. The discussion can begin.

Now I turn to the other example of how messages about

symbols issue from the Vatican only to be decoded here as messages about ethics. The celebration of the Eucharist is central to Catholic dogma. If this gets bowdlerized, then the tendency which Herberg describes for denominations to become social compartments empty of distinguishing doctrines will have worked its way right through the modern world. Historic, sacramental Catholicism will have faded out.

To introduce the problem, I take Pope Paul's Encyclical letter *Mysterium Fidei* (1965). Here he refers, as his reasons for pastoral concern and anxiety, to current disquieting views on the Eucharist. Among these, he notes that it is not

right to be so preoccupied with considering the nature of the sacramental sign that the impression is created that the symbolism – and no one denies its existence in the most holy Eucharist – expresses and exhausts the whole meaning of Christ's presence in this sacrament. Nor is it right to treat of the mystery of transubstantiation without mentioning the marvellous change of the whole of the bread's substance into Christ's body and the whole of the wine's substance into his blood, of which the Council of Trent speaks, and thereby to make these changes consist of nothing but a 'trans-signification' or a 'transfinalization', to use these terms. Nor, finally, is it right to put forward and to give expression in practice to the view which maintains that Christ the Lord is no longer present in the consecrated hosts which are left over when the sacrifice of the Mass is over. (Paul VI, 1965 : 7–8)

Here is a doctrine as uncompromising as any West African fetishist's that the deity is located in a specific object, place and time and under control of a specific formula. To make the deity inhabit a material object, whether shrine, mask, juju or piece of bread, is ritualism at its starkest. The condensation of symbols in the Eucharist is staggering in its range and depth. The white circle of bread encompasses symbolically the cosmos, the whole history of the Church and more, since it goes from the bread offering of Melchisidech, to Calvary and the Mass. It unites the body of each worshipper to the body of the faithful. In this compass it expresses themes of atonement, nourishment and renewal. Such intensive condensation is hard for anyone to stomach who has had a highly verbal, personal upbringing. But this is not all.

Symbolizing does not exhaust the meaning of the Eucharist. Its full meaning involves magical or sacramental efficacy. If it were just a matter of expressing all these themes, symbolizing and commemorating, much less blood and ink would have been spilt at the Reformation. The crux of the doctrine is that a real, invisible transformation has taken place at the priest's saying of the sacred words and that the eating of the consecrated host has saving efficacy for those who take it and for others. It is based on a fundamental assumption about the human role in religion. It assumes that humans can take an active part in the work of redemption, both to save themselves and others, through using the sacraments as channels of grace – sacraments are not only signs, but essentially different from other signs, being instruments. This touches on the belief in *opus operatum*, the efficacious rite, whose very possibility was denied by Protestant reformers. In Catholic thought there is an economy of mediation through the Church, through the sacraments and especially through the Mass as the Eucharistic counterpart of Calvary. Dr Francis Clark goes to the root of this question in his admirable survey, *The Eucharistic Sacrifice and the Reformation*, from which I quote now. Protestantism rejected mediation equally through the instrument of things as through the instrument of persons. For Luther, and above all later teachers,

there was no place for any created reality to mediate to men God's salutary action, nor for the active sharing by men in the dispensation of grace. His cardinal objection against the traditional doctrine of the sacrifice of the Mass was that it was a 'work', something which belonged to that whole order of instrumental mediation and of man's active participation in the economy of grace that was anathema to the Reformer . . . The celebration of the Lord's supper was a promise and a testament of that pardon to the individual communicant; it could not 'do' anything for others nor could it 'offer' anything to God . . . In the *Babylonian Captivity* he insisted:

God does not deal, nor has he ever dealt with man in any other way than by the word of his promise. So too we can never have dealings with God in any other way than by faith in that word of promise. (*Werke*, Weimar, vi: 516, 521)

This radical opposition of inner 'word' to sacramental 'work' is the theological key to the understanding of the storm of hostility to the Mass which swept across Europe. (Clark 1960: 106–7)

He goes on to quote Dr J. Lortz, saying:

It was a direct attack on the traditional sacramental concept, that is, against the objectivity of the divine life operative in the Church's liturgy. Here the resolution of Christianity into a religion of inner feeling was achieved at the very point at which its victory would have the greatest impact. Here was assailed the secret centre of the Church's unity . . . For the Catholic Church, it was not the attack on the Papacy that was the most fateful event which has happened in the Reformation, but the emptying out from her Mysteries of the objective source of power. (*Die Reformation im Deutschland*, 2nd edn, i, p. 229, quoted in Clark, 1960: 107)

No wonder that Pope Paul is worried by contemporary theologians who whittle down the Eucharist's meaning and who by ambiguous terms such as 'trans-signification' and 'trans-finalization' threaten to reduce it from an efficacious source of power to a mere symbol. Two years after his Encyclical, the Sacred Congregation of rites issued an *Instruction on the Eucharistic Mystery* (1967). Here it propounds four different modes of Christ's presence, recognizes them all, but exalts above all the presence in the Eucharist. Christ is present in the body of the faithful gathered in his name. He is present in his Word. He is present in the person of the minister, 'and above all under the species of the Eucharist. For in this sacrament Christ is present in a unique way, whole and entire, God and man, substantially and permanently.' This is the message that is sent out. By the time it reaches the faithful it is emasculated more than somewhat. For the writers of popular catechisms and prayer books have evidently been through Bernstein's personal upbringing. They prefer to expatiate verbally on their inner feelings, at a cosier, more intimate level. My comparison with primitive religions would probably disgust them. Great magical acts of worship, which make humble and noble analogs congruent in ever more inclusive patterns, leave them cold. So we find that the *New Catechism*, in the chapter on the Eucharist, gives to the doctrine

of the real presence only as much attention as it gives to t
commemorative aspect of the rite. It says rather more about t
Eucharist as a thanksgiving, about the togetherness of the peop
who celebrate it, and the symbol of the common meal a
nourishment. The doctrine of the transformation of the brea
into divine body is played down and the other modes of Chris
presence (particularly the 'Word') played up (Higher Catechetic
Institute, Nijmegen, 1967: 332–47). They can't take it, the Dut
bishops who issued this catechism and the open-minded Engli
teachers who seize on it as a watered-down expression of a fai
that has practically lost meaning for them. The mystery of t
Eucharist is too dazzlingly magical for their impoverish
symbolic perception. Like the pygmies (I say it again, since th
seem often to pride themselves on having reached some high pe
of intellectual development) they cannot conceive of the deity
located in any one thing or place.

But, if my interpretation of Bernstein's research is right, va
unlettered flocks scattered over the globe do not share t
disability. By reason of their positional upbringing and soc
experience they are capable of responding profoundly to symbc
of orientation and boundary. I will show in Chapter 5 that th
already use their own bodies as symbolic analogs for thinki
about society and the universe. They respond less strongly
verbal exposition. They probably feel less need for personal jus
fication by good works. What is too strong meat for their pastc
is their natural food. 'The hungry sheep look up and are not fee
There is no question now that the flocks are neglected by joll
hunting parsons bent on pleasure. But there seems to be a ca
for arguing that serious, well-intending pastors misundersta
the need for a nourishing food, because it does not seem to s
their own digestive systems. But this would still not be pitchi
the case against them strongly enough. There is no person who
life does not need to unfold in a coherent symbolic system. T
less organized the way of life, the less articulated the symbo
system may be. But social responsibility is no substitute f
symbolic forms and indeed depends upon them. When ritualis
is openly despised the philanthropic impulse is in danger

defeating itself. For it is an illusion to suppose that there can be organization without symbolic expression. It is the old prophetic dream of instant, unmediated communication. Telepathic understanding is good for brief flashes of insight. But to create an order in which young and old, human and animal, lion and lamb can understand each other direct, is a millennial vision. Those who despise ritual, even at its most magical, are cherishing in the name of reason a very irrational concept of communication.

I have dared to compare Christian ritual with magic and primitive notions of taboo. I am aware that the argument will hardly serve to recommend ritual to the non-ritualist. Yet his contempt both for magic and rules of impurity is based on ignorance. The drawing of symbolic lines and boundaries is a way of bringing order into experience. Such non-verbal symbols are capable of creating a structure of meanings in which individuals can relate to one another and realize their own ultimate purposes. Learning and perception itself depend on classifying and distinguishing. Symbolic boundaries are necessary even for the private organizing of experience. But public rituals which perform this function are also necessary to the organizing of society. One could suppose that industrial society, which is organized by economic exchange, does not need to be activated by symbols necessary to create solidarity in small communities. This might account in straight Durkheimian terms for the withering away of interest in ritualism today. It does not at all account for the lack of ritual in some tribal societies. But if the argument works for ourselves there is a dreary conclusion for those who turn to good works to solve problems about their own identity. They are liable to be frustrated on every count. First, it would seem that they must give their good causes over to the bureaucratic energies of industrial organization, or they will have no effect. Second, although any office or clinic is capable of being organized by positional symbolic patterns, since these people are incapable of appreciating the value of symbolic behaviour they will never be able to arrange their personal relations so that a structure of non-verbal symbols can emerge. We all know the seminar chairman who takes a different seat every week so that no symbols of authority or precedence can invest the spatial relations of the group. Some of us may even know the small publisher's office where the office boy has to be consulted now and again about the quality of a book and where the manager makes the tea because it is felt that solidarity requires continuous confusion of roles. An anthropologist told me that his inhibition against exercising authority was so strong that his first fieldwork had to be made extremely difficult by his refusal to employ a servant. These very people, who prefer unstructured intimacy in their social relations, defeat their wish for communication without words. For only a ritual structure makes possible a wordless channel of communication that is not entirely incoherent.

The confirmed anti-ritualist mistrusts external expression. He values a man's inner convictions. Spontaneous speech that flows straight from the heart, unpremeditated, irregular in form, even somewhat incoherent, is good because it bears witness to the speaker's real intentions. Either he is not a man who uses speech as a façade to conceal his thought, or on this occasion there was no time for polishing it up: incoherence is taken for a sign of authenticity. In the same way, leaders in a Pentecostal church compete to demonstrate their holiness by 'talking with tongues', that is by pouring out a stream of incoherent speech. The more unintelligible, the more evident to the congregation that the gift of tongues is present. At the same time the anti-ritualist suspects speech that comes in standard units, polished with constant use; this is the hard coin of social intercourse, not to be trusted as expressing the speaker's true mind.

In rejecting ritual forms of speech it is the 'external' aspect which is disvalued. Probably all movements of religious renewal have had in common the rejection of external forms. In Europe Manicheeism, Protestantism and now the revolt of the New Left, historically they all affirm the value of the follower's inside and of the insides of all his fellow members, together with the badness of everything external to the movement. Always we find bodily symbolism applied, from the values placed on internal and external parts of the body, on reality and appearance, content and form, spontaneity and established institutions. David

Martin has recently written of contemporary religious existentialists in these terms:

> Radicals tend to reject 'religion' by comparison with the gospel. Religion is a complex of institutions built around an idol 'God' who is falsely regarded as an existence alongside other existences. The proper use for the word 'God' is to refer to the qualitative aspect of all existence. Religion obscures Him in forms and formulae, ritualizes him sacramentally when in truth, He can only be known experimentally and experientially. Only thus can He become true for the individual person. Bound up with false religion is morality, understood as a body of rules rather than as genuine personal responses to the uniquely situational character of moral choice ... The existentialist movement expresses an ageless tension between the experiential and the formalized, the objective and the personal, the individual and the institutional. (1965: 180–81)

Why the elect always carry in themselves a confidence in their own inner purity and their capacity for direct, unmediated access to God is something best accounted for by the psychoanalysts. But it is a paradox of this study that those who most readily despise ritual should not be exempt from the longing for non-verbal communication. Melanie Klein, writing of the close contact between the unconscious of the mother and of the child, said:

> However gratifying it is in later life to express thoughts and feelings to a congenial person, there remains an unsatisfied longing for an understanding without words – ultimately for the earliest relation with the mother. (Klein, 1963: 100)

And again, of an infant's attitude to the breast of his mother:

> I would not assume that the breast is to him merely a physical object. The whole of his instinctual desires and his unconscious fantasies imbue the breast with qualities going far beyond the actual nourishment it affords.
>
> Footnote: All this is felt by the infant in much more primitive ways than language can express. When these pre-verbal emotions and phantasies are revived in the transference situation, they appear as 'memories in feelings', as I would call them, and are reconstructed and put into words with the help of the analyst. (Klein, 1957: 5)

If it is true that we are moved all our lives by longings for an ideal, impossible harmony derived from memories of the initial union with the mother in the womb, then it is understandable that we should also idealize non-verbal communication. Alas for the child from the personal home who longs for non-verbal forms of relationship but has only been equipped with words and a contempt for ritual forms. By rejecting ritualized speech he rejects his own faculty for pushing back the boundary between inside and outside so as to incorporate in himself a patterned social world. At the same time he thwarts his faculty for receiving immediate, condensed messages given obliquely along non-verbal channels.

4   Grid and Group

It is illuminating to consider ritual as a restricted code. But more problems arise in applying this insight than I am ready to handle. Bernstein argues that the restricted code has many forms; any structured group that is a group to the extent that its members know one another very well, for example in cricket, science or local government, will develop its special form of restricted code which shortens the process of communication by condensing units into pre-arranged coded forms. The code enables a given pattern of values to be enforced and allows members to internalize the structure of the group and its norms in the very process of interaction. Much of the writings and conference proceedings of anthropologists, or of every other body of scholars, would have to be classed as ritualistic or restricted code in so far as the citing of fieldwork, the reference to (often impossible) procedures, the footnotes etc., are given as pre-coded items of social interaction. Allegiances, patronage, clientship, challenge of hierarchy, assertion of hierarchy and so on, these are being obliquely and silently expressed along the explicit verbal channels. If this is so, then Bernstein, by working within the broad framework of a dichotomy of restricted and elaborated codes, is at the stage of Durkheim when he distinguished mechanical and organic solidarity, or of Maine, distinguishing societies governed by contract or by status. As he himself says, the distinction between restricted and elaborated codes must be relative within a given culture or within the speech forms of a given group. Thus the question of whether there are primitive cultures in which all speech is in the restricted code is meaningless, since it ascribes absolute value to the definition. Bernstein would suppose that in any social group there are some areas of social life more responsible for policy decisions and more exposed to the need to communicate with outsiders. Therefore in any tribal system he would expect to find some people who had been forced to develop a more elaborated code in which universal principles can be made explicit and meanings detached from a purely local context. I am not convinced of this myself. If the situations requiring policy decisions were only part of a repetitive cycle it would be possible to discuss them fully in terms of pre-organized units of speech. Only the need for innovation in policy would call forth the effort to use an elaborated speech code. This question poses intriguing problems of method for the ethno-linguists. But it is not central to my theme. More pertinent is how to use the idea of the restricted code to interpret different degrees of ritualization.

If ritual is taken to be a form of restricted code, and if the condition for a restricted code to emerge is that the members of a group should know one another so well that they share a common backcloth of assumptions which never need to be made explicit, then tribes may well vary on this basis. One can well suppose that the pygmies might never get to know each other very well. Their social intercourse might be likened in intensity and structure to that of the provisioners of a French seaside resort who move down from Paris in June to open their shops and hotels for the tourist season. They know each other quite well, there is a field of common assumptions to be sure, but it by no means exhausts their interests. They could be expected to develop a restricted code with reference to their local concerns. So we can also suppose that the pygmies and the Persian nomads who join their respective hunting or pastoral camps for a season and may not necessarily be together for next year, use one restricted code for those of their common concerns to which an enduring social structure corresponds, and variant forms of restricted code for communication within their own families. This analogy from speech codes suggests good reason for the poverty of ritual forms in the two cases. It fits the Durkheimian premise that society and God can be equated: to the extent that society is confused in its structure of relations, to that extent is the idea of God poor and unstable in content.

The restricted code is used economically to convey information and to sustain a particular social form. It is a system of control as well as a system of communication. Similarly ritual creates solidarity and religious ideas have their punitive implications. We would expect this function to be less and less important the less is effective social coherence valued. We cannot therefore be surprised that the pygmies have not developed the punitive aspects of religion. They are content with a minimal level of organization. Here again a range of comparison is suggested which would predict something about the presence and absence of ritualism in human societies. We need some way of comparing the value set on organization and social control. It is all very well to illustrate my theme by references to exotic tribes. At some point the problem of comparison must be brought under control. Not only is it dubious practice to compare preachers with pygmies. It is just as dubious to compare hunters with pastoralists, or hunters in Africa with hunters in Australia. I will try to control this problem of cultural variation by staying as much as possible within a given culture. But first, the task is to adapt Bernstein's diagram of systems of family control. It was designed to reflect the increasing influence of the division of labour in industrial society on two variables, speech and techniques of control. Our first step, then, is to eliminate the effect of the division of labour by choosing slightly different variables. Since Bernstein's work relates to the structure of London families it is concerned with personal face-to-face relations. Consequently it needs very little adaptation for tribal society. His two lines measure different aspects of what he calls positional behaviour in families. Where the division of labour has least effect, the speech code and the control system support a differentiated structure of relations in the family. If we want to follow his work closely we must first do violence to the subtlety of his thought. In Bernstein's diagram (p. 50), speech codes respond to the pressure exerted from the decision-making areas at the centre-top of industrial society for more and more verbal articulateness.

Family control systems respond to the same set of pressures demanding children capable of mastering intellectual abstractions concerning human behaviour. His quadrant was designed to show how the two responses are not produced in the same combination in all sectors of industrial society. The area of maximum structuring of social relations in the family is on the left: the area of maximal openness and freedom from structuring is on the right. In the bottom right the individual emerges as free as possible from a system of socially structured controls. His diagram illustrates some effects of a single pressure to move from the positional to the personal control system. The vertical line expresses changes in the use of speech. It shows the possibility of speech being used as an intensifier of positional control, with this possibility diminishing as the central pressure to be intellectually, verbally and symbolically free of the local positional structure develops. The people who have been freed most completely from structured personal relations are among those most involved in the complexity of modern industrial structure. Inevitably this model has to be dismantled to be adapted to tribal society. In what follows we are working with only a very crude and limping parody of his idea.

The task can be simplified if we recall what it is essentially that he is doing. He is deriving cosmology from control systems, or rather showing how cosmology is a part of the social bond, according to the following principles. First, any control system, since it has to be made reasonable (be justified, validated or legitimated as Weber put it), must appeal to ultimate principles about the nature of man and of the cosmos. This applies even at the family level. Second, that the control system interacts with the media of control (speech, ritual). Third, that certain consistencies hold between the coding of the medium and the character of the control system. That they should match is a long-run prediction. In a short run the transition process might obscure the match. Our task starts therefore by identifying the control aspects of the cosmology.

Somewhere far away from the level of the English family and home, some machinery is grinding out a set of social pressures.

Naked power is decently clothed and made legitimate. Its demand to be made legitimate reaches into the most intimate recesses, even into the dealings the English mother has with her own child. She learns to assert her control in certain ways and to justify her authority by reference to general principles. The child is thus indoctrinated into the assumptions of his society. His curiosity is checked or roused, his expectations for himself are set in the most hidden way – not by the overt doctrines handed out, but by what is left implicit. Bernstein exposes two implicit world views carried in our styles of speech. He finds them generated in two distinguishable systems of control. To match his exercise, we should look to systems of control and the hidden assumptions which validate them. We are not ready to deal with how the media vary. This is for the next chapter. So, leaving aside speech codes, at this stage I would need to produce a comparison of control systems which will contrast an entirely personal form of relationships, un-structured by fixed principles, with a system equivalent to his positional family. We can concentrate, it seems, upon the interaction of individuals within two social dimensions. One is order, classification, the symbolic system. The other is pressure, the experience of having no option but to consent to the overwhelming demands of other people. Consider order first. Social relations demand that categories be clarified and orientations given. Order is the basic requirement for communication. It could conceivably be possible to compare symbolic systems according to the clarity of definition given to the categories used. There is a hint of such a programme in the first pages of *Primitive Classification*.

For us, in fact, to classify things is to arrange them in groups which are distinct from each other and are separated by clearly determined lines of demarcation . . . At the bottom of our conception of class there is the idea of a circumscription with fixed and definite outlines. Now one could almost say that this conception of classification does not go back before Aristotle . . . Not only has our present notion of classification a history, but this history itself implies a considerable pre-history. It would be impossible to exaggerate, in fact, the state of indistinction from which the human mind developed. Even today a considerable part of our popular literature, our myths, and our religions is based on a fundamental confusion of all images and ideas. They are not separated from each other, as it were, with any clarity ... If we descend to the least evolved societies known, those which the Germans call by the rather vague term *Naturvölker*, we shall find an even more general mental confusion. (Durkheim and Mauss, 1903: 5–6)

The authors go on to compare this weakness of definition to the growth of consciousness in the individual from childhood to adulthood: distinctions when they first appear are fragmentary and unstable; only gradually does a steady circumscription of elements of experience lead to classification. However this is not the basis for a comparison of classification systems which I propose to use here. I shall take it as axiomatic that the clarity of bounding of different categories within the total system does not vary, or that, if it does become fuzzy here and rigid there, this is not a difference which I wish to take into account. I shall instead try to compare the overall articulation of the categories which constitute a world view. A classification system can be coherently organized for a small part of experience, and for the rest it can leave the discrete items jangling in disorder. Or it can be highly coherent in the ordering it offers for the whole of experience, but the individuals for whom it is available may enjoy access to another competing and different system, equally coherent in itself, from which they feel free to select segments here and there eclectically, not worrying about the overall lack of coherence. Then there will be conflicts, contradictions and uncoordinated areas of classification for those people. In effect, loss of coherence results in a narrowing of the total scope of the classification system. We can therefore take the scope and coherent articulation of a system of classification as one social dimension in which any individual must find himself. I shall call it grid.

As Durkheim himself has powerfully argued, any given classification system is itself a product of social relations. Bernstein's example of the positional family above shows people putting pressures on one another in terms of classifications. When the pressures are strong and when they uphold a set of classifications, then a process of mutual reinforcement is at work.

Such a social system is likely to remain stable, unless counter-pressures develop from outside or unless new knowledge weakens the credibility of the classifications. In either case, the social change will be wrought in the other dimension, that of action or pressure. To draw the dimension of grid vertically up from zero towards more and more comprehensive articulations allows us to consider what absence of classification would mean. The zero would represent a blank, total confusion with no meaning whatever. Rulelessness could be anomy, the suicide's doubt. It could be the mystic's moment of dissociation when all classifications are in abeyance. It could also represent, as the quotation from *Primitive Classification* suggested, the child's first undifferentiated awareness. To distinguish among these possibilities a little, let us separate the publicly accepted classification system from the private one. An increasingly coherent but entirely private system of classification would point away from communication with others, eventually to madness. This world of private thought we draw downwards from zero.

On the horizontal axis, draw pressure, increasing from zero to the right. At zero, no demands are made on the individual. He is free of pressure. This means he is alone. But another case would have to be located on the vertical line. When pressures and counter-pressures completely balance out, the point of indecision would be recorded here. It is the moment before conversion and commitment. Towards the right he is increasingly under the bond of other people. For reasons which will be clear later, I call the tendency towards the maximum personal control the line of group. A child's life starts far along that line (since he is completely controlled by others) and low on the line of grid: as he grows he may be progressively freed from personal pressures and progressively indoctrinated in the prevailing classification system. If he is clever at internalizing the categories and their implications, he can turn them to his own defence against personal tyranny. He can even use them to tyrannize. To allow for this, we can extend the horizontal line from zero to the left. On this side the individual has escaped all pressure from other people. He is exerting pressure on them.

Diagram 4: Grid and Group

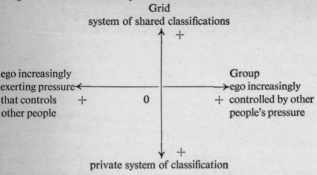

Grid
system of shared classifications

ego increasingly
exerting pressure ←————————————→ ego increasingly
that controls   +   0   + controlled by other
other people   people's pressure

Group

private system of classification

Although the public grid of classifications is used by other people to control the individual, he can evade it if ever the insulation breaks down. The mutual reinforcing of grid and group keep the system stable only if it is perfectly insulated. But perfect insulation is rare and there is some scope for change. We have now in hand a device which could consider social change as a dynamic process. We can see the individual under strong pressure to accept a system of classification which degrades him and commits him to a life of servitude. We could assess the other options open to him, and the relative weight of competing pressures. But this is not the exercise I am attempting. Our problem is to find some relation between cosmological ideas and characteristics of social relations. I shall argue that several systems which spread in different patterns across the diagram are liable to develop recognizable trends in the way that the universe is constituted. The first task is to investigate more closely the properties of the chart.

Above the horizontal line is the area of public classification. The social system will always be centred here. Close to the line and below it lie the fringe elements, the marginal sectors of society: the more to the right they are found, the weaker their option not to be exploited by others to the left operating the public system of classifications; towards the left and zero are the voluntary outcastes, tramps, gipsies, rich eccentrics, or others who retain their freedom, at a cost. This line across the page separates the area of conformity from innovation. Given the way we have defined the vertical dimension we are not suggesting that anyone is dreaming up new conceptual systems from scratch. What is private and innovatory is the way the common cultural categories are articulated. Progress further down that line to greater coherence of the private philosophy depends on an accompanying isolation from social pressures. Beyond a certain point of originality the thinker can give up any reasonable expectation of his ideas being received. This follows from the relation between grid and group above the horizontal line of zero. The framework of institutional life and the distribution of power is the result of a long-term adaptation between social pressures and classification. The big push that changes classification must be big enough to redistribute power as well. To the far right the fringe area of private thought is socially null. It is under more pressure than it can exert. Far to the left it is in high public esteem: hordes of people to the far right would be applauding each new impulse emanating from the far lower left. It is worth pausing to consider how a person can be located in that quadrant. A musician can innovate, a painter, inventors and writers too. If his idea be ignored, he is still on the right. For most of his long working life the Flemish painter, James Ensor, endured that fate and revenged himself on the public which denied him honour by cruel caricatures. If successful, though, the innovator may see the public system of classification change in his own lifetime. If he wants to stay original, he will have to keep thinking of something new to surprise them with, or devise a technique for maximizing the unexpected, as John Cage has done for his music. To remain free of the public system of classification, the person needs above all not to covet its rewards. Every glance he cocks towards the prize-giving juries makes him vulnerable to their criticisms and liable to be sucked into the general grid. Thus, though it is difficult to stay there, it is possible for people to pass in their lifetimes through different points in the bottom left quadrant.

The bottom right quadrant can be filled for infancy. Here is the personal family in which the child is controlled by being made sensitive to an inventory of his parent's aches and pains: no public system of classification is used to explain the universe and his place in it, but (theoretically at least) he is taught to develop a classificatory system of his own. However, publicly known categories implicitly underline their behaviour and he is quick to deduce them as he grows older. It is surely impossible for an adult to accept heavy social pressure and yet to develop a privately articulated philosophy. If he wishes to have intellectual privacy he must inevitably achieve a solitary state, and so the tendency would be for such a person to move across from right towards the vertical line of no control.

This leads us to considering further the relations between the distribution of power and the coherence of public classifications. It is axiomatic that a steady pattern of control is needed for a coherent system of classification. The more distinguishable places in the control system and the more these are co-ordinated into a lasting hierarchy of responsibilities, the more the public classification system differentiates its categories. So a society spread across the diagram from the highest point mid-way between public grid and group on the right and across to some high point mid-way at the top left is a complex social system. Time depth and corporate institutions are implied in that pattern. Conversely, one political shake-up makes many classifications irrelevant and drags down the coherence of the symbolic system; the expectation of continuing change sets the level lower still. A society that is spread across the diagram at a low level of classification is likely to become one that is continually subject to political upheaval and a changing profile for the distribution of authority. This will be important for our theme.

We should now examine the different ways these dimensions organize our material. Some tribal systems will be spread mostly through the top right-hand side of the diagram without showing on the left. A classic instance of high classification which anthropologists would recognize are the Tallensi of the Volta Region of Ghana as described by Meyer Fortes in the colonial period. Here the public system of rights and duties equips each man with a full identity, prescribing for him what and when he eats, how he grooms his hair, how he is buried or born. Most Tallensi, probably all, are under pressure from the others. The chiefs and priests are no exception. The person whose soul is in revolt is regarded as abnormal and needing special ritual curing (Fortes, 1959). In this society piety is the order of the day, piety towards senior kinsmen and piety to the dead, even though the ancestors are seen as aggressive punishers. The only enemy is the rank outsider, bound by no ties of clanship. A few miserable old women outlawed as witches are either hounded from village to village or merely tolerated. Who knows their thoughts? If they are totally mystified by the public grid which rejects them we could locate them below the horizontal line, though far to the right where options are weakest. I will argue later that a social system characterized by high classification would display the same cosmological bias. Strong grid and strong group will tend to a routinized piety towards authority and its symbols; beliefs in a punishing, moral universe, and a category of rejects.

Any bureaucratic system which is sufficiently secure and insulated from criticism will tend to think the same way. This is the monastic life, or the military society. Most clearly it is the stable tribal system discovered by anthropologists in Africa in the colonial era just before and after the Second World War. It is no accident that a functional analysis produced an equilibrium model of primitive society at that time. For the colonial regime itself provided the insulation and protection from the effects of war and famine. It tended to freeze the native social systems into patterns of reinforcement and stability.

However the effect was not the same in Central Africa as it was in Ghana. Here the long nineteenth-century wars with Arabs and other slave-raiders had already broken up the local social structures before the colonial freeze came down. The tribes in the region around Lake Nyasa are very differently characterized in the writings of the 1950s when labour migration, cash crops, and taxation accelerated the process of change. Here we also find small communities. But as to grid they come much lower on the line of coherent classification than the

Tallensi. Their culture promises them contradictory rewards and holds out impossible goals. They believe that it is good to be loyal and obedient and never to split a village into factions. They also believe that the proper ambition of every man is to become head of his own village – impossible without disloyalty and friction. They put immense pressure on one another and strive incessantly to define and close the circle of their friends. Accusations of witchcraft are the political idiom of out-casting and re-definition of social boundaries. The broad, normative concept of a human being for whom moral obligations are binding is contrasted with that of the man-eating witch. To convict a rival of witchcraft is to finish him politically. This is the second of the main types of social environment I shall refer to throughout the book. For convenience I shall call it small group. It is a social system which clusters low on the right side of the diagram. Its members know one another and can count their ranks and prospects of promotion. They are not conscious of remote control by leaders located far to the left. Hemmed in and face to face, their destiny is in their own hands and they meet it with intrigue and jealousy. The contrast of small group with the previous case of high classification ranges over many aspects. For example, high classification requires a well-defined category of rejects and anomalous persons. But small group broadens the category of potential rejects to include the whole range of acquaintance, male, female, kinsman and unrelated.

The third type to distinguish from these two is the society which spreads widely across our diagram instead of being tidily clustered on the right. The leaders in the small-group case are down in among their community, struggling against their peers. In this third case which I shall call strong grid, the leaders are remote powerful beings, rarely seen face to face. We shall need to deal separately with the social environment of the leaders and of those who are subject to them.

During the colonial period, for reasons we have suggested, anthropology was much concerned with the properties of corporate groups and with rights and duties transmitted down enduring channels of control. Colonialism itself checked internal evolution and limited tribal political systems to the mere replacement of personnel in a fixed pattern of office. But research in newly independent countries, and above all in newly discovered New Guinea, has focused attention on what is called the network of links a man has to a circle radiating out from himself. In a complex society, networks are the minimum level at which social relations can be investigated. They are the sustaining base line of social ties from which corporate institutions arise. But if corporate organization is so weak that each man has to muster support *ad hoc* for every venture, a system of networks and temporary action-sets may describe the way the whole society functions. Philip Gulliver has summarized ably the problems of description and analysis which the anthropologist faces in such societies (1971). I wish to concentrate on one of two possible variations of the network. In the case which Philip Gulliver himself describes, of the Ndendeule in Tanzania, no person stays in any position of eminence over others, there are no chiefs and there are no effective boundaries to the spread of the open network in all directions. For each man the meanings of society are centred upon himself but the meanings are the same for him as for others. By contrast, in other variants, it is possible for leaders to become effective and to entrench their power in their lifetime at least. Such a leader will gather his own network of allegiances powerfully round himself and create a centre of force for the rest of society. The Big Man system, as it is called in New Guinea, is found all over the world, in Indonesia, among northern Californian Indians, in the Philippines. I take it for my fourth social type, to contrast with the other two patterns. Its interest is the wide spread across the diagram of grid and group at a low level of classification. Success breeds. There are few overriding community interests to check the leader's impetus. The greater his influence, the more support he attracts. A positive feedback propels him further out to the left; it increases the subjection of his followers, so they move to the right. If his success in wealth and war encourages him, he may end by eroding their existing system of obligations and become a law unto himself. Then the inevitable trend would be to lower the level of classification for everyone in his orbit. He has made their lineages and ancestral shrines less meaningful for them than his own favour. The big categories however, solvency, worth, equity, remain as containers into which a changing synthesis of meaning is poured from year to year. However, the leader has to reckon with rivals creeping near to him in eminence. The world of his peers is a sparse and fluctuating scene of coalitions. Each is bent on success. If they are realistic, their followers recognize that right goes with might and line up accordingly. This type of social system in its various stages has now been frequently and well described. There are many more examples from New Guinea. The interesting difference between them is the range within which the competition of Big Men must use existing corporate institutions or can override them and in doing so attaches large parts of the public system of classification to the whims of the Big Men themselves.

We have now distinguished three types of social environment: high classification, small group, strong grid which includes the heroic society of competing Big Men and that of their followers. The latter come low on the vertical line of classification because coherence is achieved only at some very general level of abstraction which is compatible with the syncretizing rivalry of distant giants. But the spread across the diagram expresses the strong control which these people experience. Recruited and harnessed to a competition which seems to hold glittering rewards for all, they find themselves trying to work a complex system of rules. In the name of the rules the Big Men justify their demands. Whether it be rules of monetary exchange, debt and credit, or rules of etiquette and hospitality, the system constitutes an oppressive grid. Londoners too know what this can mean. As a system of control industrial society is impersonal. Some more than others feel their lives controlled, not by persons, but by things. They wander through a forest of regulations, imponderable forces are represented by forms to complete in triplicate, parking meters, inexorable laws. Their cosmos is dominated by objects of which they and fellow humans are victims. The essential difference between a cosmos dominated by persons and one dominated by objects is the impossibility of bringing moral pressures to bear upon the controllers: there is no person-to-person communication with them. Hence the paradox that some of the people whose metaphysics are most fuzzy and who respond only to very diffuse symbols – in short, who in their cosmology are most like pygmies and Arizona peyotists – are those who are much involved in certain sectors in industrial society. To this paradox I shall return.

For the leaders who have spiralled down far to the left the same impersonal rules of exchange are made like rungs on a ladder of promotion. The Big Men live in a world of noble pacts, hard bargains, dastardly betrayals and revenges. Apart from the exotic cases given, there are examples nearer home. Our ancient Anglo-Saxon vengeance and inheritance laws defined a set of responsible kin radiating from each particular individual. The Norse sagas expressed a corresponding world view.

With these four social types distinguished it will be possible to show that they generate distinctive cosmologies. The system of control is validated by a typical bias in the system of belief. These tendencies are the subject of this book, for they make their own typical demands on the media of expression and thus produce natural systems of symbolic behaviour. A brief summary of the types of belief would go as follows. With high classification, piety and sacralized institutions, strong boundaries between purity and impurity; this is the prototype original Durkheimian system in which God is Society and Society is God, where all moral failings are at once sins against religion and the community. With small group there is less confidence in the power of God to protect the faithful, a dualist cosmology reckons with the power of demons and their allies; justice is not seen to prevail. Strong grid tends to a pragmatic world view, sin is less understood than shame for loss of personal honour, face or solvency. In the first type a profit and loss calculus applies to the spiritual economy of the whole community; strong grid focuses on the honour of the individual, the number of supporters he can summon up, the control he has over his women folk. Strong grid divides between the heroic society of the Big Men, and the recurrent millennial tendencies of their subjects. Finally the positions near and around zero should be specially noticed. When public classification and pressures are withdrawn or cast aside, the individual left alone with himself develops a distinctive cosmology, benign and unritualistic.

As Durkheim suggested, this experience is the beginning of consciousness, with all the emotional force that that implies. The sense of escape from others and of self-discovery is possible with any shift towards the left of the diagram. Out here, especially below the vertical line, where the individual is articulating his own classificatory system, the thinker does not see his fellow human beings as the principal determinants of social life. Fellow humans do not put their imprint on the world as models of controlling influence. In consequence the cosmos is not anthropomorphic. There is less call for articulate forms of social intercourse and no need for a set of symbols with which to send and receive specific communications. Thus we have already identified one area of the diagram in which there will be less regard for ritual. Furthermore, it suggests another dimension which is not on the diagram, that lying between density and sparsity. When populations are sparse and social relations infrequent, interrupted and irregular, a person does not have the impression of inhabiting a man-dominated world. What preoccupations about his fate he may entertain concern drought, pasture, livestock, movements of game, pests or growth of crops. He is controlled by objects, not persons. Objects do not respond to personal modes of approach. Fellow humans are fellow sufferers.

It is tempting to try to assimilate whole cultures to the general outlook of individuals dropping to near zero. But sparsity conceals too many variables; better to stick to those on the diagram. There is ample material there for explaining the similarity between the world view of pygmies in the Ituri forest and that of certain Londoners deeply implicated in industrial society. First we should turn to the media of social relations. If the pattern of social relations put their stamp upon speech forms, as Bernstein's work shows, they no doubt put a pattern upon non-verbal forms of communication as well. If the speech forms thus produced themselves control the kind of social responses possible in a given social environment, we should expect the usage of the body for communication to exert a parallel constraint.

5   The Two Bodies

The social body constrains the way the physical body is perceived.
The physical experience of the body, always modified by the
social categories through which it is known, sustains a particular
view of society. There is a continual exchange of meanings between the two kinds of bodily experience so that each reinforces
the categories of the other. As a result of this interaction the body
itself is a highly restricted medium of expression. The forms it
adopts in movement and repose express social pressures in manifold ways. The care that is given to it, in grooming, feeding and
therapy, the theories about what it needs in the way of sleep
and exercise, about the stages it should go through, the pains it
can stand, its span of life, all the cultural categories in which it is
perceived, must correlate closely with the categories in which
society is seen in so far as these also draw upon the same culturally processed idea of the body.

Marcel Mauss, in his essay on the techniques of the body
(1936), boldly asserted that there can be no such thing as natural
behaviour. Every kind of action carries the imprint of learning,
from feeding to washing, from repose to movement and, above
all, sex. Nothing is more essentially transmitted by a social
process of learning than sexual behaviour, and this of course
is closely related to morality (ibid.: 383). Mauss saw that the
study of bodily techniques would have to take place within a
study of symbolic systems. He hoped that the sociologists would
co-ordinate their approaches with those of perception theory as
it was being developed then by Cambridge psychologists (ibid.:
372). But this is as far as he got, in this gem of an essay, to sug-

gesting a programme for organizing the study of 'l'homme total'.

Whereas Mauss was concerned to emphasize the culturally learnt control of the body, other scholars, before and after, have noticed unconscious correspondences between bodily and emotional states. Psychoanalysis takes considerable account of what Freud called 'conversion' of the emotional into the physical condition. This insight has had immense therapeutic and theoretical importance. But the corresponding lessons have not yet been drawn for sociology. Many scholars have made shrewd observations of unconscious bodily enactment. I cite as an isolated example Rudolph Otto's idea of 'natural magic':

> Modes of behaviour exhibiting some simple analogy and carried out quite unreflectively and without any basis in theory . . . It may be noticed on any skittle-alley or bowling-green. A bowler aims and plays his ball, wishing it to run true and hit the jack. He watches eagerly as it rolls, nodding his head, his body bent sideways, stands balancing on one leg, jerks over violently to the other side as the critical point is reached, makes as though to push the ball on with hand or foot, gives a last jerk – and the end is reached. Its hazards past, the ball rolls safely into position. (Otto, 1957: 117–18)

Such observations do not remotely approach a general sociological theory such as Mauss was seeking. Nor, in my opinion, does Edward Hall's contemporary research in bodily symbolism amount to a theory. *The Silent Language* (1959) deals with well-observed differences of convention in the use of space, time and gesture. But that is all. There is no attempt at a hypothesis by which cultural variations can be explained. Lévi-Strauss's monumental analysis of the structure of symbolism does not come much nearer to the programme enjoined by Mauss. For though he promises to incorporate into the analysis of symbolic structures culturally specialized attitudes to mobility and immobility, eating and fasting, cooking and not cooking and so on, he is seduced away from this programme by his interest in a universal structure of thought common to all mankind. He seems to offer a perspective in which social controls on the human body can be included in a vast psycho-sociological analysis of controlling schemata (*Mythologiques*, 1964, 1966, 1968), but he cannot come up with anything interesting about cultural variations (which are local and limited) since his sights are set on what is universal and unlimited to any one place or time. His analysis of symbolism lacks an essential ingredient. It has no hypothesis. Its predictions are impregnably, utterly irrefutable. Given the materials for analysis (any limited cultural field), given the techniques of analysis (selection of pairs of contrasted elements) – there is no possibility of an analyst going forth to display the structures underlying symbolic behaviour and coming home discountenanced. He will succeed, because he takes with him a tool designed for revealing structures and because the general hypothesis only requires him to reveal them. He is not asked to correlate particular kinds of symbolic structures with predicted social variables. He will inevitably bring out of his research a series of structured oppositions which are all finally resolvable into the contrast of culture with nature. Lévi-Strauss has given us a technique. It is for us to refine it for our own problems. To be useful, the structural analysis of symbols has somehow to be related to a hypothesis about role structure. From here the argument will go in two stages. First, the drive to achieve consonance in all levels of experience produces concordance among the means of expression, so that the use of the body is co-ordinated with other media. Second, controls exerted from the social system place limits on the use of the body as medium.

The first point is a familiar principle of aesthetics. The style appropriate to any message will co-ordinate all the channels along which it is given. The verbal form, syntactically and lexically, will correspond to the kind of situation to be expressed; tautness, slackness, slowness, speed, will give further information of a non-verbal kind; the metaphors selected will add to the meaning, not diminish it.

Then let us give praise to the Lord, brethren, by our lives and by our speech, by our hearts and by our voices, by our words and by our ways. For the Lord wants us to sing Alleluia to Him in such a way that there may be no discord in him who gives praise. First, therefore, let our speech agree with our lives, our voice with our conscience. Let our words, I say, agree with our ways, lest fair words bear witness against false ways.

So preached Augustine in Carthage in the year 418. The sermon is quoted more fully by Auerbach and analysed as an example of a peculiar kind of rhetoric (Auerbach, 1965: 27–36). Augustine's problem was how to present the enormously difficult paradox of Christianity as if it were something obvious and acceptable. He tried to solve it by combining the grand sweep of Ciceronian rhetoric with robust simplicity. Cicero had taught that there are three distinct levels of style, the sublime, the intermediate and the lowly; each level was supposed to belong to its own class of subject matter, so that some situations and things were noble in themselves and should be spoken of in the sublime manner and others too humble for anything but the lowly style. The unquestioned assumptions on which such values could be assigned imply a restricted code. But Augustine argued that Christianity turned all previous values around: the most humble objects became sublime. He therefore proceeded to detach the styles of rhetoric from classes of things and acts and related them firmly to the social relations holding between speaker and listener. The sublime style was for rousing emotions, the intermediate for administering praise or blame and the lowly for teaching. It is wholesome for anthropologists struggling to interpret ritual to recall this long tradition of inquiry into the relation of style to subject matter and social relations. Auerbach's book is devoted to the study of what changes in the traditional form of discourse occurred under the impact of Christian ideas. Note too that the lowly style was called *lingua humilis*, related to *humus*, soil, and meaning literally low, low-lying and of small stature. Christian teaching attacked the established pattern of values by mixing the humble style with the sublime. So the manner itself in which the message was given added more of the same meaning. In the same way Barthes (1967) writes of a French editor of a revolutionary journal opening his editorial with a sprinkling of obscenities. They were only relevant to the matter being discussed in that their style had the same revolutionary impact. In any kind of communication whatever, if more than one band is being used, ambiguity would result if there was no smooth co-ordination of meanings. Hence we would always expect some concordance between social and bodily expressions of control, first because each symbolic mode enhances meaning in the other, and so the ends of communication are furthered, and second because, as we said earlier, the categories in which each kind of experience is received are reciprocally derived and mutually reinforcing. It must be impossible for them to come apart and for one to bear false witness to the other except by a conscious, deliberate effort.

Mauss's denial that there is any such thing as natural behaviour is confusing. It falsely poses the relation between nature and culture. Here I seek to identify a natural tendency to express situations of a certain kind in an appropriate bodily style. In so far as it is unconscious, in so far as it is obeyed universally in all cultures, the tendency is natural. It is generated in response to a perceived social situation, but the latter must always come clothed in its local history and culture. Therefore the natural expression is culturally determined. I am merely relating what has long been well known of literary style to the total bodily style. Roland Barthes gives a contemporary description of style as a non-verbal channel of meaning.

Imagery, delicacy, vocabulary spring from the body and the past of the writer and gradually become the very reflexes of his art. Thus under the name of style a self-sufficient language is evolved which has its roots only in the depths of the author's personal and secret mythology, that sub-nature of expression where the first coition of words and things takes place, where once and for all the great verbal themes of his existence come to be installed whatever its sophistication. Style has always something crude about it: it is a form with no clear destination, the product of a thrust, not an intention, and, as it were, a vertical and lonely dimension of thought ... It is the private portion of the ritual, it rides up from the writer's myth-laden depths and unfolds beyond his area of control. (Barthes, 1967: 16, 17)

Such bodily styles as we are writing of arise spontaneously but are also interpreted in the same spontaneous way. Read the impression made by John Nelson Darby, a leader of the Brethren movement in the 1820s:

A fallen cheek, a bloodshot eye, crippled limbs resting on crutches, a seldom-shaved beard, a shabby suit of clothes and a generally neglected person, at first drew pity, with wonder to see such a figure in a drawing-room ... With keen logical powers, he had warm sympathies, solid judgment of character, thoughtful tenderness and total self-abandonment. He before long took Holy Orders, and became an indefatigable curate in the mountains of Wicklow. Every evening he sallied forth to teach in the cabins, and roving far and wide over mountains and amid bogs, was seldom home before midnight ... He did not fast on purpose, but his long walks through wild country and indigent people inflicted on him much severe deprivation ... Such a phenomenon intensely excited the poor Romanists, who looked on him as a genuine 'saint' of the ancient breed. The stamp of heaven seemed to them clear in a frame so wasted by austerity, so superior to worldly pomp and so partaking in their indigence ... I was at first offended by his apparent affectation of a careless exterior. But I soon understood that in no other way could he gain equal access to the lower and lowest orders, and that he was moved not by asceticism, nor by ostentation, but by a self-abandonment fruitful of consequences. (Quoted from Francis William Newman, in Coad, 1968: 25, 26)

Note how the word self-abandonment occurs twice in this passage. Nelson Darby through all his life wrote against organization as if it were the greatest betrayal and sin for the Brethren to organize themselves into a Church (Coad, op. cit.: 127).

Now for the second stage of the argument. The scope of the body as a medium of expression is limited by controls exerted from the social system. Just as the experience of cognitive dissonance is disturbing, so the experience of consonance in layer after layer of experience and context after context is satisfying. I have argued before that there are pressures to create consonance between the perception of social and physiological levels of experience (Douglas, 1966: 114–28). Some of my friends still find it unconvincing. I hope to bring them round by going much further, following Mauss in maintaining that the human body is always treated as an image of society and that there can be no natural way of considering the body that does not involve at the same time a social dimension. Interest in its apertures depends on the preoccupation with social exits and entrances, escape routes and invasions. If there is no concern to preserve social boundaries, I would not expect to find concern with bodily boundaries. The relation of head to feet, of brain and sexual organs, of mouth and anus are commonly treated so that they express the relevant patterns of hierarchy. Consequently I now advance the hypothesis that bodily control is an expression of social control – abandonment of bodily control in ritual responds to the requirements of a social experience which is being expressed. Furthermore, there is little prospect of successfully imposing bodily control without the corresponding social forms. And lastly, the same drive that seeks harmoniously to relate the experience of physical and social, must affect ideology. Consequently, when once the correspondence between bodily and social controls is traced, the basis will be laid for considering co-varying attitudes in political thought and in theology.

This approach takes the vertical dimension of experience more seriously than the current trend in the structural analysis of symbolism which requires meanings to be found horizontally, as it were, by the relation of elements in a given pattern. It is what Rodney Needham, following the phenomenologists and Bachelard, has called analysis in depth (1967: 612). In linguistics it may well have been a blind alley to seek to interpret the selection of sounds by reference to their physical associations. Structural analysis of language has foregone considering whether sibilants have onomatopoeic associations with running water, snakes and the like. Structural analysis should, perhaps, not be interested in the psychological significance, or social, of a particular symbol. But when anthropologists apply this technique to the analysis of ritual and myth, the vertical references to physical and social experience are generally slipped in, without apology, as extensions of the total structure. Surely the account we take of the vertical dimensions of analysis must be made explicit, in order to understand the basis of natural symbols. A study of anti-ritualism must focus on the expression of formality and informality. It seems not too bold to suggest that where role structure is strongly defined, formal behaviour will be valued. If we were to proceed to analyse a range of symbolism under the general opposition of formal/informal we would expect the formal side of every contrasted pair to be valued where role structure is more dense and more clearly articulated. Formality signifies social distance, well-defined, public, insulated roles. Informality is appropriate to role confusion, familiarity, intimacy. Bodily control will be appropriate where formality is valued, and most appropriate where the valuing of culture above nature is most emphasized. All this is very obvious. It goes without saying that any individual moves between areas of social life where formality is required and others where it is inappropriate. Great discrepancies can be tolerated in differently defined sectors of behaviour. And definition may be in terms of time, place or dramatis personae, as Goffman showed when he considered what criteria women use to decide when it is and is not permissible to walk in the street in slippers and hair nets (1959: 127). Some individuals groom their whole appearance to the same pitch of formality, while others are careful here and relaxed there. James Thurber once remarked that if some writers dressed as carelessly as they wrote they would be prosecuted for indecency. This range of personal experience can build up a demand for more and more formal symbols of distance and power where a crescendo is held appropriate – and vice versa a diminuendo in symbols of formality on other occasions. The need and ability to switch from the one set of symbols to its contrary is often discussed in terms of reversals. But here I am concerned not with reversal, but with the possibility of a fading out of control, a general détente, and its symbolic expression.

So far we have given two rules: one, the style appropriate to a message will co-ordinate all the channels; two, the scope of the body acting as a medium is restricted by the demands of the social system to be expressed. As this last implies, a third is that strong social control demands strong bodily control. A fourth is that along the dimension from weak to strong pressure the social system seeks progressively to disembody or etherealize the forms of expression; this can be called the purity rule. The last two work together, so I shall deal briefly with purity first, before illustrating how they dictate the bodily media of expression.

Social intercourse requires that unintended or irrelevant organic processes should be screened out. It equips itself therefore with criteria of relevance and these constitute the universal purity rule. The more complex the system of classification and the stronger the pressure to maintain it, the more social intercourse pretends to take place between disembodied spirits. Socialization teaches the child to bring organic processes under control. Of these, the most irrelevant and unwanted are the casting-off of waste products. Therefore all such physical events, defecation, urination, vomiting and their products, uniformly carry a pejorative sign for formal discourse. The sign is therefore available universally to interrupt such discourse if desired, as the editor of the revolutionary journal mentioned above knew. Other physiological processes must be controlled if they are not part of the discourse, sneezes, sniffs or coughs. If not controlled, formal framing-off procedures enable them to be shorn of their natural meaning and allow the discourse to go on uninterrupted. Lastly, and derived from the purity rule, are two physical dimensions for expressing social distance; one is the front-back dimension, the other the spatial. Front is more dignified and respect-worthy than back. Greater space means more formality, nearness means intimacy. By these rules an ordered pattern is found in the apparently chaotic variation between diverse cultures. The physical body is a microcosm of society, facing the centre of power, contracting and expanding its claims in direct accordance with the increase and relaxation of social pressures. Its members, now riveted into attention, now abandoned to their private devices, represent the members of society and their obligations to the whole. At the same time, the physical body, by the purity rule, is polarized conceptually against the social body. Its requirements are not only subordinated, they are contrasted with social requirements. The distance between the two bodies is the range of pressure and classification in the society. A complex social system devises for itself ways of behaving that suggest that human intercourse is disembodied compared with that of animal creation. It uses different degrees of disembodiment to express the social hierarchy. The more refinement, the less smacking of the lips when eating, the less mastication, the less the sound of breathing and walking, the more carefully modulated the laughter, the more controlled the signs of anger, the clearer comes the priestly-aristocratic image. Since food takes a different place in different cultures this general rule is more difficult to see at work in table manners than in habits of dress and grooming.

The contrast of smooth with shaggy is a member of the general set of symbolic contrasts expressing formal/informal. Shaggy hair, as a form of protest against resented forms of social control, is a current symbol in our own day. There is no lack of pop-sociology pointing a moral which is fully compatible with my general thesis. Take the general run of stockbrokers or academics, stratify the professional sample by age; be careful to distinguish length of hair from unkempt hair; relate the incidence of shagginess in hair to sartorial indiscipline. Make an assessment under the division smooth/shaggy of other choices, preferred beverages, preferred meeting-places and so on. The prediction is that where the choices for the shaggy option cluster, there is least commitment to the norms of the profession. Or compare the professions and trades one against another. Those which are aiming at the centre top, public relations, or hair dressing, and those which have long been fully committed to the main morality, chartered accountants and the law, they are predictably against the shaggy option and for the smooth drink, hair style, or restaurant. Artists and academics are potentially professions of comment and criticism on society: they display a carefully modulated shagginess according to the responsibilities they carry. But how shaggy can they get? What are the limits of shagginess and bodily abandon?

It seems that the freedom to be completely relaxed must be culturally controlled. What do we make, therefore, of the fact that most revivalist movements go, in an early phase, through what Durkheim called 'effervescence'? Emotions run high, formalism of all kinds is denounced, the favoured patterns of religious worship include trance or glossalalia, trembling, shaking or other expressions of incoherence and dissociation. Doctrinal differentiation is deplored. The movement is seen to be universal in potential membership. Generally the stage of effervescence gives way to various forms of sectarianism or to the growth of a religious denomination. But it is not true that effervescence must either be routinized or fizzle out. It is possible for it to be sustained indefinitely as the normal form of worship. The only requirement is that the level of social organization be sufficiently low and the pattern of roles sufficiently unstructured. We do not have to look for strain, change, deprivation or tension to account for effervescent religious forms. They can be found in steady state religions. Talcott Parsons's definition of the contrast of structured and unstructured helps to identify those tribes which celebrate social solidarity by the greatest abandonment of conscious control.

In a highly structured situation there are a minimum of possible responses other than the ones required by the norms of the situation; adaptation is carefully defined; and usually the situation is not very confusing psychologically. (1956: 236)

The less highly structured, the more the value on informality, the more the tendency to abandon reason and to follow panics or crazes, and the more the permitted scope for bodily expressions of abandonment. We can summarize the general social requirements for religious formality and informality, that is for ritualism on the one hand and effervescence on the other, as follows:

SOCIAL DIMENSION	SYMBOLIC ORDER
A *Conditions for Ritualism*	
(i) high classification, strong control	condensed symbolic system; ritual differentiation of roles and situations magical efficacy attributed to symbolic acts (e.g. sin and sacraments)
(ii) assumption that interpersonal relations must be subordinate to public pattern of roles	symbolic distinctions between inside and outside
(iii) society differentiated and exalted above self	symbols express high values set on control of consciousness

103

B *Conditions for Effervescence*

(i) weak control by grid and group	diffuse symbols; preference for spontaneous expression, no interest in ritual differentiation; no magicality
(ii) little distinction recognized between interpersonal and public patterns of relations	no interest in symbolic expressions of inside/outside
(iii) society not differentiated from self	control of consciousness not exalted

The second case provides the social conditions for a religion of ecstasy as distinct from a religion of control. Ethnographic reading suggests that the attitude to consciousness is not merely neutral, as I have written it here, but that there is a positive affirmation of the high value of consciousness whenever the corresponding social structure demands control of individual behaviour. So we tend to find trance-like states feared as dangerous where the social dimension is strongly controlled. According to my general hypothesis, the inarticulateness of the social organization in itself gains symbolic expression in bodily dissociation. The religious cult of trance is material especially suitable to the present thesis. When it occurs at all, the reporting tends to use very vivid language, the ethnographer trying to convey something of ecstasy or fear. The general atmosphere and mood are on record. It is usually quite clear, when trance takes place, what the onlookers think about it. Among the Samburu trance occurs regularly, but is not part of religion, no beliefs are connected with it (Spencer, 1965: 263). Among Nuer, it is held to be dangerous; among Dinka it is held beneficent. Trance is a good point on which to test my hypothesis. The prediction is that, as trance is a form of dissociation, it will be more approved and welcomed the weaker the structuring of society.

Raymond Firth has distinguished three kinds of trance states. To his classification I will add a fourth class. His series runs from minimum to maximum control by the human group of an invading spirit. First, there is spirit possession in which a human passively loses control to the spirit. The latter is in power. The friends of the possessed person try to pacify it and send it away. Then there is spirit mediumship, in which the invading spirit speaks through the possessed person, and the group try to get occult information and power from it. Third is shamanism. Here the spirit is to a large extent domesticated and made to do the will of the human host (Firth, 1967: 296). Significantly, perhaps, an entirely distinct category of trance has been omitted. It may happen that the human person loses consciousness, but the state is not regarded as undesirable or dangerous; the onlookers may make no attempt to control and try to use, nor to change the state, pacify or send away the invading influence. They assume that it is a channel of benign power for all. This is the positive cult of trance as such. I would only expect it to take place in the main morality cult where social life comes closer to the zero. Let me give two vividly described examples which are worth quoting.

The Western Dinka pay cult to the divinity, Flesh, which manifests itself in a red light. A hymn begins: The Flesh kindles like fire. Yet Flesh confers judgement and truth, it shows itself in a cool heart, peacefulness, harmony and order. Godfrey Lienhardt describes a sacrifice thus:

> As the invocations proceeded, the legs of some of the masters of the fishing-spear began to tremble, a trembling which came from the quivering of the upper leg and thigh. This, it was said, was the divinity Flesh, which was beginning to awaken (*pac*) in their bodies.
>
> The divinity Flesh was specially manifested in this quivering of the legs and thighs, which sometimes spreads further to the whole body. The masters of the fishing-spear continued to invoke with the mounting force of Flesh in them. They did not become 'hysterically' possessed, as do those who are possessed by free-divinities. Two young men, members of these spear-master clans though not themselves masters of the fishing-spear, then also began to show signs of the 'awakening' of Flesh in them. They were much less controlled, and their arms and legs were soon trembling violently. One was sitting, one standing, and both gazed blankly before them with their eyes open and turned slightly upwards. It was possible to go up to them and stare closely into their faces without either's registering that he saw anything.
>
> Nobody at this stage paid much attention to them; it was said that when thus possessed by Flesh in the homestead, they were safe, and

that if the condition persisted for too long the women would put an end to it by venerating the divinity Flesh in their bodies, giving those possessed by it their bangles, and kissing their hands. Later, women did kiss the hands of these possessed men, but bangles were not offered.

As the invocations increased in speed and intensity an older man became overpowered by the divinity Flesh, and staggered about among the invoking masters of the fishing-spear, slapping and leaning on the bull-calf and jostling people. His behaviour was that of a man who is very giddy. At this stage visiting masters of the fishing-spear were in turn pouring libations of milk from a ring-decorated gourd over the peg to which the calf was tethered. Each made his libation, kissing his own hands before and after handling the gourd of the Flesh, the gourd reserved for libations to this divinity. When one master of the fishing-spear returned from this act of veneration, he told me that his own Flesh was 'waking up', though he behaved with self-control for the rest of the ceremony.

The mounting or awakening of the divinity Flesh in the body seems to be a well-known sensation to all adult male members of spear-master clans. Females do not have it. A Christian Dinka of the Pakwin clan told me that he dared not draw near when a beast was being sacrificed to his clan-divinity, as the awakening of the Flesh in him brought on a sensation of faintness, which might result in his falling unconscious. (Lienhardt, 1961: 136–8)

The veneration of the divinity Flesh in the bodies of those who manifest it, at least from the ethnographer's viewpoint, is the most solemn religious act of these people.

Here is an account of a possession cult in which the invading spirit is not feared, not pacified or driven off, not made use of as an oracle, nor for healing specific sickness. The visitation of the spirit is respectfully venerated, the presence is sought for its own sake, for an unmediated form of communion between a god and his worshippers.

But what can I say of the social structure of the Western Dinka which would relate their cult of trance to my argument? Nothing but a close examination of grid and group as they apply to these Dinka, and to other Dinka and to other Nilotes in their region, will be relevant. It should turn out that these Dinka are less closely controlled by social constraints than other peoples sharing the same cultural postulates but differing in their attitude to trance. This I will broach in the next chapter.

After this, it is easy to recognize a rather more ambivalent attitude to trance. According to Lorna Marshall the !Kung Bushmen of the Nyae-Nyae region of the Kalahari desert consider total unconsciousness as dangerous, but intermediate stages of semi-conscious trance they hold to be the proper means of procuring health and blessing. Their ceremonial curing dance is the one religious act which has form and in which the people are united. Its purpose is general: to cure sickness and drive away evil. The men wear rattles; the women clap loudly and sharply.

The clapping and stamping are of such precision that they give the effect of a well-played battery of percussion instruments producing a solid structure of intricate rhythm. Above the percussion sounds, the voices of the men and women weave together in parts, singing the 'medicine songs' ... After several dances have been danced the medicine men begin to cure. Almost all the !Kung men are medicine men. They do not all choose to practise, for one reason or another, but there are always several in a band who are active. Medicine men receive no rewards other than their inner satisfactions and emotional release. I know that some of them feel a deep responsibility for the welfare of their people and great anxiety and concern if their curing fails, and a corresponding satisfaction if it prevails. Others of them appear to be less concerned about the people whom they try to cure and more inwardly turned. When the medicine men are curing, all of them experience varying degrees of self-induced trance, which includes a period of frenzy and a period of semi-consciousness or deep unconsciousness. They may become stiff or froth at the mouth or lie still as if in coma. Some of them habitually remain in trance for only a short time, others for hours. One man used to remain in a semi-trance for most of the day following a dance ... After the curing has been going on for some time, medicine men begin to reach their state of frenzy. They no longer go around to the people, their spasms of grunting and shrieking become more frequent and violent, their stomachs heave, they stagger and sway. They rush to the fire, trample it, pick up the coals, set fire to their hair. Fire activates the medicine in them. People hold them to keep them from falling and beat out the flames ... they may fall into deep unconsciousness or sink down semi-conscious, eyes closed, unable to walk.

The medicine men who have not reached their full frenzy or who have passed through it attend to those who are in it. The !Kung believe that at such a time the medicine man's spirit leaves his body and goes out . . . They call this 'half-death'. It is a dangerous time and the man's body must be watched over and kept warm. The medicine men lean over the one who is in trance. They shriek and gurgle. They blow in his ears to open them. They take sweat from their armpits and rub him. Some fall over him in trance themselves and are in turn rubbed and cared for by the others. The women must sing and clap ardently while the man is in deep trance. He needs the good medicine of the music to protect him.

The curing dance draws people of a Bushman band together into concerted action as nothing else does. They stamp and clap and sing with such precision that they become like an organic being. In this close configuration – together – they face the gods. They do not plead, as they do in their individual supplications, for the favour of the divine, all-powerful beings, and do not praise them for their goodness. Instead, the medicine men, on behalf of the people, releasing themselves from ordinary behaviour by trance and overcoming fear and inaction, throw themselves into combat with the gods and try to force them with hurled sticks and hurled words to take away the evils they might be bringing. (Marshall, 1962: 248–51)

Here, though trance is courted and held to be benign in effect, it is not regarded as altogether safe. Several new intensive studies of other Bushmen bands are now being made. These may give an opportunity for the comparisons within a given social environment which I am hoping will test my thesis. I would ask for study of the positive cult of trance among different Bushmen groups to work out detailed variations along the lines of social control by grid and group. As to the cult of trance itself, I would ask about the way the roles are distributed: whether it is practised by all, by all males or by all females, by specialists chosen by birth or by trained and initiated specialists. About the trance state, I would be interested in attitudes to varying degrees of bodily control and abandonment, their danger, whether to the person in trance or to others. About the beneficent powers attributed to trance, I would ask how general or how specific they are held to be. I would expect more highly specialized trance roles, more sense of danger in trance, more specific, narrowly defined benefits attributed to trance where social control by grid and group is more intense. Referring back to the diagram of the last chapter, shifts towards zero should allow the body a fuller range of expression for a smaller range of intentions. Its full abandon is made available in this direction.

Where trance is not regarded as at all dangerous, but as a benign source of power and guidance for the community at large, I would expect to find a very loosely structured community, group boundaries unimportant, social categories undefined, or distant control but impersonal rules strong. Take for example Calley's account of West Indian sects in London (1965). The rule of limiting the comparison to persons interacting in the same social field would certainly allow me to compare their bodily techniques of expression with Pentecostalists in Trinidad or Jamaica where they share a cultural tradition. But I should also be able to compare them with the transport workers and others with whom they interact, at work or in pubs and labour exchanges in London. Calley finds that the theory of compensation for poverty and distress does not explain the religious behaviour of West Indians, who were materially richer in London than at home. But his account of these London Pentecostal churches gives a clear picture of the fluid, ever-shifting social units to which individuals were so loosely attached. A founding minister of a new Church had a hard task to maintain a stable congregation. Rivalries easily led to a splitting into two or more groups. The temporary tenure of their meeting-places (ibid.: 107) corresponded to the temporary tie of individuals with their work (ibid.: 140). Calley implicitly makes the comparison with the tendencies to fission and fusion in primitive society. But I shall simply compare their state of social flux with the steady allegiances of the Londoners among whom they lived. For the Pentecostalists, as the name implies, the greatest gift of the Holy Spirit is the gift of tongues, which gives insight, foresight and healing. But, paradoxically, the gift of tongues is recognized by totally inarticulate gabbling of Allelujahs. The more he is inarticulate the more proof that the speaker is unconscious and not in control of what is being imparted to him.

Inarticulateness is taken as evidence of divine inspiration. So also are 'dancing in the Spirit', involuntary twirling and prancing, and involuntary twitching and shuddering taken to be a sign of blessing (ibid.: 80–81).

I imagine the English in this same environment spend their Sunday mornings polishing their cars, or neatly trimming their lawns and window boxes, or correctly repeating the Lord's Prayer in unison. Compared with these English, these West Indians are weakly structured in several senses. Their groups are ill-defined; they have no common provenance from a single country of origin, no common organization; amongst themselves their social categories are weakly formed, their allegiance to local groupings undetermined; in relation to the other inhabitants of their London environment they have few close or permanent contacts with the representatives of power and authority. There are few West Indian school teachers, policemen, social workers. By contrast the non-West Indians with whom they come into more than casual contact are more clearly categorized and have more permanent attachments to jobs and homes, and often a more secure relation with the sources of control. On my thesis, it is expected that the London West Indians should favour symbolic forms of inarticulateness and bodily dissociation more than the Londoners with whom they interact. Their religion is not a com-pensation, but a fair representation of the social reality they experience. If this general correlation between social and bodily forms of control is to be a useful insight, it must be made clear that it does not predict anything about the occurrence of physio-logically defined trance states. It is a prediction about attitudes to bodily dissociation and whereas the attitudes can be assessed by the ethnographer, the degree of bodily dissociation has to be taken in the first instance as a construct of the local culture. It would be inconsistent with the whole argument about the cul-turally conditional experience of the body if we seemed to be asserting something absolute about the place of trance in religion. What I am saying is that the full possibilities of abandoning con-scious control are only available to the extent that the social system relaxes its control on the individual. This has many implications for the deprivation approach to religious behaviour. For religious movements which take this form are expressing social solidarity without differentiation: the question of whether this state occurs as a result of deprivation must be considered separately in each instance.

We can add this case to other ranges of symbolic behaviour in which a tendency to replicate the social situation is observed. Van Gennep first discerned the common form in all ceremonies of transition (1960). Where the transfer from one social status to another is to be expressed he noted how material symbols of transition were inevitably used and also how the rite itself takes the form of preliminary separation from and re-integration into the community. As this applies across cultural boundaries it is a natural symbolic form. At a more profound level, the social experience of disorder is expressed by powerfully efficacious symbols of impurity and danger. Recently I have argued that the joke is another such natural symbol (1968c). Whenever in the social situation, dominance is liable to be subverted, the joke is the natural and necessary expression, since the structure of the joke parallels the structure of the situation. In the same sense, I here argue that a social structure which requires a high degree of conscious control will find its style at a high level of formality, stern application of the purity rule, denigration of organic process and wariness towards experiences in which control of consciousness is lost.

A friend, criticizing the first version of this argument, reproached me for trying to stand Freud on his head. I am indeed insisting that the social imagery which the body carries be recognized. This is not reversing or taking anything away from psychoanalytic theory but expanding the social perspective in which it is set. Psychoanalysis takes account of a very restricted social field. It makes of parents and siblings the social framework into which all subsequent relationships are slotted. The restriction gives it great theoretical elegance and power. But it is difficult to extend its categories in a controlled way to the wider experience of society. Those who have tried a macro-application of psychoanalytic theory to nations and cultures can interpret imaginatively

111

as they will; anyone else is free to come up with a contrary diagnosis of the same events. Grid and group are offered as tools for describing in a more controllable fashion the way that social pressures reach an individual and structure his consciousness. The vertical distance between zero and the most coherent set of classifications offered by his culture is the range of sublimation possible in it. The span across the diagram from left to right represents the possibilities of frustration for those with the fewest options. A society huddled together in the right quadrant, with strong face-to-face pressure and low classification, will go on stoking the sibling jealousies of childhood. Strong group and strong grid working together will uphold the strength of paternal authority. It should be interesting to place the classic psychoses upon the diagram. But this is a digression.

The main burden of this chapter is to take up the theme of the book's title. Natural symbols will not be found in individual lexical items. The physical body can have universal meaning only as a system which responds to the social system, expressing it as a system. What it symbolizes naturally is the relation of parts of an organism to the whole. Natural symbols can express the relation of an individual to his society at that general systemic level. The two bodies are the self and society: sometimes they are so near as to be almost merged; sometimes they are far apart. The tension between them allows the elaboration of meanings.

6   Test Cases

At a stage in her life when she had cut herself free from social
ties, Simone Weil reproved the ancient Israelites for their adherence to rule, for the legalism of the priests and their rejection
of the Dionysian mystery cults (1951). But it was all very well
for her to make the judgement. It would be impossible for the
leaders of an occupied but still resisting nation to adopt an effervescent form of religion. To expect them to stop preaching a stern
sexual morality, vigilant control of bodily boundaries, and a corresponding religious cult would be asking them to give up the
political struggle. So long as they were set upon that, the choice
was no more open to them to worship God with wine, song and
dance than it was open to Simone Weil herself to make a strict
religious commitment when she had relaxed her own commitment to society.

The principle of symbolic replication of a social state leads us
to a different view of revivalist movements among the poor and
oppressed. Compensation theory too glibly explains by reference
to physical suffering and deprivation of civil and economic rights.
Then it finds this explanation does not cover the throng of well-
to-do women who so often predominate in these movements. So
it turns to sexual frustration. In the following passage Norman
Cohn adopts a simple Freudian approach to explain the female
element in millenarian movements:

... emotional frustration in women of means and leisure but without
social function or prestige. Throughout the history of Christianity
this circumstance has contributed to the rise of revivalist movements
and it still does so today. What ideal such a movement sets itself seems

to depend chiefly on personal factors – in the first place on the particular personality of the prophet, which will appeal only to certain types of women. The antinomian and erotic millenarism of the Brethren of the Free Spirit does however indicate one recurrent possibility . . . Do comparable movements occur in societies where sexual life is less guilt-ridden than it has usually been in Christendom? (1962: 41)

The answer is yes: the tendency to celebrate sexual promiscuity is not a response to repression; it is more likely to be found where repression is least in evidence. Cohn also mentions as alternative causes, political oppression and sudden catastrophe (see Chapter 9 below).

My explanation of effervescent religious revivalism is tidier since it uses only one hypothesis to predict its occurrence both among the poor and deprived and among the females of the rich and privileged classes, and also its likely development following catastrophe. In all cases, it is the lack of strong social articulation, the slackening of group and grid which leads people to seek, in the slackening of bodily control, appropriate forms of expression. This is how the fringes of society express their marginality. It is enough to say that the experience of a certain kind of structuring of society gets expressed in a certain way, without invoking the emotionally distracting principle of deprivation. In relation to established authority, this area of the social structure is the wilderness from which prophets and new cults are observed to arise. The collection of essays on *Spirit Mediumship and Society in Africa* (ed. Beattie and Middleton, 1969) is a rich mine of examples. Robin Horton makes this very point in his contribution on the main varieties of spirit possession in Kalabari religion. He contrasts possession by big spirits and minor spirits.

Possession by the big spirits is subject to a public scrutiny and control which discourages any departure from a traditionally-prescribed content. Its principal significance is that it reminds people, sometimes at recurrent intervals and sometimes at times of communal crisis, of the presence and attributes of the spirits, and of the values they support. Its general setting leaves little room for individual innovation on the part of the medium. Possession by the minor water-spirits, on the other hand, is virtually free from public scrutiny and control. Although it too serves to remind people of the presence and attributes of the spirits, it has a much wider range of significance. Thus it provides a means of personal adjustment for those whose ascribed position in society is excessively irksome to them. It also provides the occasion for both narrative and dramatic art. Finally, it provides a means for the propagation of new ideas about the world. In all these contexts, the impress of individual innovation is very evident.

These differences are, I think, fairly readily explained. First of all, doctrines relating to the founding heroes and the big local water-spirits occupy a crucial place in the community's world view. They both interpret, validate and indicate means for the perpetuation of the established order of society and ecology. Any change in such doctrines is potentially a grave threat to the established order of things. Hence there is continual public scrutiny to insure that no such change takes place. Since possession by the big spirits gives dramatic reminders and illustrations of these doctrines, it must be included in the scrutiny.

Doctrines relating to the minor water-spirits are, by contrast, rather marginal to the community's world-view. Collectively, it is true, these minor spirits have an important part to play in the explanation of the peculiarities of individual life-courses. But no one spirit is involved with more than a few individuals. Again, these minor spirits are by definition the owners of distant creeks with which the community is not practically concerned. Particular spirits of this class, then, are important neither to the community as a whole nor to any considerable section of it. Hence doctrines concerning them are free from the scrutiny and control applied to doctrines concerning the big spirits. And this freedom extends to possession by them.

One consequence is that possession by the minor water-spirits comes readily under the influence of a variety of desires and needs other than those concerned with the explanation, prediction and control of the world. Thus it becomes caught up in the struggle to find a way round uncongenial ascriptions of status, and again in the struggle to elaborate forms of both narrative and dramatic art. Another consequence is that the individual 'carrier' is free to make his personal contribution to the content of possession: a freedom which has been amply exploited in both of these contexts.

This freedom also makes possession by the minor water-spirits a promising channel for innovations in belief and doctrine which may eventually come to assume importance in the community at large. Since the utterances of these spirits on the heads of their carriers are virtually free from public scrutiny and control, they can serve as vehicles of new ideas which would be scotched at birth if they came from one of the big spirits. Remember how, during the time of the first Christian conversions, it was a minor water-spirit that went about telling people to join the churches since the day of the *oru* was over.

Through the same freedom, it is even possible that these marginal spirits may provide the material for renewing and readapting the very core of the community's world view. We don't have much evidence on this; but one case is suggestive. This is the case of the spirit carried by one of the two men in our sample of people possessed by 'women's *oru*'. This spirit was first announced as the owner of a distant creek, far away from the community's own sphere of interest and operations. Later, it came to announce itself as a controller of local waters who acted together with the established bit water-spirit Duminea. During a visit by a Shell prospecting party, it assumed responsibility for the oil resources of the neighbouring creeks; and when oil was found, the community gave it the credit for the discovery. For some time now, the community has been on the brink of treating it as an object of public cult.

With this case in mind, we may look again at some of the myths which tell how village heroes originally came out of the world of the water-people to live with men. I have already offered an intellectualist interpretation of such myths. But it would seem possible to supplement this with a more historical (though highly speculative) interpretation. It is that the heroes, and other big spirits, were originally introduced to the community as minor water-spirits on the heads of *oru kuro* people; and that they stayed incubating on the sidelines until, at some time of social upheaval and change requiring new interpretative concepts, they came out to make grander claims for themselves. Elsewhere, I have described how in former times Kalabari got rid of spirits who seemed to have no further usefulness to the community. We may have a clue here as to how they got themselves new spirits to meet new challenges to their way of life. (Horton, op. cit.: 45-7)

In his Malinowski lecture on Spirit Possession (1966) Ioan Lewis applies the useful distinction between the main morality cult and peripheral cults: he finds that people who are peripheral to the central focus of power and authority tend to be possessed by spirits who are peripheral to the main pantheon and whose morality is dubious. So the allocation of spiritual powers reflects the location of people along a dimension from the centre to the margins. So women subject to their husbands, serfs subject to their masters, indeed any in a state of subjection, constitute his category of the peripheral. For lack of a hypothesis about why these people should incline towards cults of bodily dissociation, the argument insidiously slides towards deprivation as the explanation and means of recognizing peripheral possession cults. But what about the Bog Irish of London? The argument is unable to deal with the many cases of people who are obviously and consciously deprived, and yet do not react in the predicted way.

It is no accident that women so often form the main membership of possession cults. The social division of labour involves women less deeply than their menfolk in the central institutions – political, legal, administrative etc. – of their society. They are indeed subject to control. But the range of controls they experience is simpler, less varied. Mediated through fewer human contacts, their social responsibilities are more confined to the domestic range. The decisions they take do not have repercussions on a very wide range of institutions. The web of their social life, though it may tie them down effectively enough, is of a looser texture. Their social relations certainly carry less weighty pressure than those which are also institutional in range. This is the social condition they share with slaves and serfs. Their place in the public structure of roles is clearly defined in relation to one or two points of reference, say in relation to husbands and fathers. As for the rest of their social life, it takes place at the relatively unstructured, interpersonal level, with other women in the case of women, with other slaves and serfs in the case of slaves and serfs. Of course I would be wrong to say that the network of relations a woman has with others of her sex is unstructured. A delicate patterning certainly prevails. But its significance for society at large is less than the significance of men's relations with one another in the public role system. A quarrel between women has not anything like the same repercussions as a quarrel between their husbands. If they want to give their social relations with one another a more central structuring, they can only do so by embroiling their menfolk. Their links with one another are only as strong as the links between the menfolk to whom they are attached. Women, serfs and slaves (especially released slaves), are inevitably pinned only weakly into the central structure of their society. A small setback can harm them more irrevocably than those whose more complex links give a better chance of recovery. Their options are few. They experience strong grid. Therefore they are susceptible to religious movements which celebrate this experience. Unlike those who have internalized the classifications of society and who accept its pressures as aids to realizing the meanings they afford, these classes are peripheral. They express their spiritual independence in the predicted way, by shaggier, more bizarre appearance, and more ready abandonment of control.

I do not wish to embark on the difference between male and female dress in expressing this difference. For it is complicated by sexual functions. Instead, consider the distinctive appearance of prophets. They tend to arise in peripheral areas of society, and prophets tend to be shaggy, unkempt individuals. They express in their bodies the independence of social norms which their peripheral origins inspire in them. It is no accident that St John the Baptist lived in the desert and wore skins, or that Nuer prophets wear beards and long hair in a fashion that ordinary Nuer find displeasing. Everywhere, social peripherality has the same physical forms of expression, bizarre and untrimmed.

It is necessary all the time to remind ourselves that we are only dealing with distant ages and remote places in order to understand ourselves. The *ceteris paribus* rule allows me to use a more local example. In noticing that Lloyd George wore his hair long and loose it is relevant only in that it was longer and looser than other members of his cabinet, not that it was longer than Roundheads or shorter than Royalists wore it two centuries earlier. It becomes extremely interesting that the verdict of two contemporaries on this long-haired premier ranges him clearly with other peripheral prophets. It is argued that he would never have come to power but for the national chaos of mid-war in 1916 and that only recurring crises of great magnitude kept him in power until 1922. Even within the political scene, he owed his promotion to a 'revolt of the cabin-boys' (Taylor, 1965: 189), a phrase which suggests a desperate abdication of reason and control to someone from the margins. He was the only politician who retired far richer than he began. The irregularity of his personal life is no secret. Not for him the main morality cult. When he made a speech he trembled and poured with sweat as if the divine afflatus was on him. Keynes, who saw him at the Peace Conference of 1919, wrote:

How can I convey to the reader, who does not know him, any just impression of this extraordinary figure of our time, this syren, this goat-footed bard, this half-human visitor to our age from the hagridden magic and enchanted woods of Celtic antiquity? One catches in his company that flavour of final purposelessness, inner responsibility, existence outside or away from our Saxon good and evil, mixed with cunning, remorselessness, love of power, that land fascination, enthralment and terror to the fair-seeming magicians of North European folklore. (Keynes, 1933: 36–7)

Here is a stirring description of a peripheral prophet-leader which corresponds closely to the ethnographic examples in respect of appearance, morality and social provenance. Having illustrated it I shall now attempt to test my hypothesis more rigorously. It requires that peoples sharing a common culture who differ radically in social organization along the specified dimensions shall show the predicted variations in religious behaviour. If I concentrate on variations in terms of the original diagram, I will try to contrast different possible patterns across the top right-hand quadrant. I will seek to contrast weaker and stronger control by grid and group. As an illustration I will compare the Nuer and Dinka, two neighbouring Nilotic tribes who are radically different in the crucial aspects of their religious behaviour. For the Western Dinka, the state of trance is treated positively as a central cult, the source of blessing and strength. For Nuer, trance is dangerous. I shall look for objectively definable social variables to account for the difference.

Those neighbouring tribes of pastoralists who raid one another, capture and enslave one another and speak related Nilotic languages are both organized on the basis of agnatic lineages.

The Nuer have been observed in a number of short visits by Evans-Pritchard and their published record is now very full. Before he wrote a large volume on Nuer religion, he produced monographs describing their ecology, political institutions and kinship and marriage, and while this work was in production, he also published numerous short articles on diverse aspects of their life. One supposes that the problem his pupil faced as ethnographer of the Dinka was delicate and complex. First, it could be tedious to recite at length the parallel chronicle of the Dinka, noting both where their practice conformed to and diverged from Nuer practice. Second, such a programme would not allow for the different perspective of a younger man, seeing the culture from the shoulders, as it were, of his teacher. This perspective might light upon different aspects, it might be more profound, and still be perfectly compatible with the earlier work on the Nuer. On the other hand, discoveries about how Dinka institutions worked might produce an embarrassing situation in which one or other or both of the two friends might find that his work discredited the findings of the other. To such a complex of delicacies we can attribute the various emphases and omissions in Godfrey Lienhardt's Dinka studies.

As far as ecological pressures and political institutions are concerned, he has adopted the alternative of summarizing very comprehensively the differences between the two peoples (1958). As far as family structure, incest, exogamy, marriage are concerned, he adopted the solution of omission. As far as religion is concerned, he adopted his own original perspective, taking the interpretation of symbolic behaviour to profound, new levels. My puzzle about whether Nuer and Dinka social experience is different in ways which would account for the difference in their symbolic order is therefore complicated by lack of detailed information about marriage regulations. From the pattern of the rest of their social and symbolic behaviour I will hazard a guess that Dinka observe less stringent, less far-reaching rules of incest and exogamy and are less consistent in using the pattern of their cattle transfers to define their categories of permitted and prohibited sexual relations.

But first let me fill in the contrast at the symbolic level, in what concerns their attitudes to spirit possession. The Nuer regard it as dangerous. Evans-Pritchard says 'Seizure of a man by a spirit may be temporary or permanent. When it is permanent the possessed person becomes a prophet . . .' Sickness is often attributed to temporary spirit possession: sacrifice is made to the spirit to appease it, and the victim, once cured, must continue to make sacrifices 'to let it know that he has not forgotten it. Otherwise it may cause trouble again.' The process of cure, apart from sacrifice, includes a séance of singing, drumming, rattling and clapping until someone close to the victim becomes possessed. In the case he describes it is the sick man's father who becomes a medium to make known the demands of the spirit. I quote:

As the singing, rattling and clapping continued, Rainen began to twitch and shake from head to foot and then suddenly leaped into the air and fell back on the floor of the hut where he lay stiff as though in a paroxysm. After lying tense and prostrate for a while he sat up, but shortly afterwards collapsed again. Then for about a quarter of an hour he threw himself wildly about the hut, writhing and twitching as though in agony. He reminded me of a hen which has had its throat cut in the Muslim way, and is thrown on the ground to die. If the people around had not broken most of his falls he might have injured himself. As it was, he complained to me on the following day of the soreness of his arms and legs. Every now and again he barked like a dog. In describing these spasms Nuer say that the spirit wrestles with the man it possesses. (1956: 36)

Note that the occasion of a spirit possessing a man is first known by the illness of the latter: in the next stage it possesses someone else with whom it wrestles violently, before it discloses its name and demands gifts. Then after some hard bargaining, the spirit is persuaded to go. The séance is in the charge of a prophet, one whose state of possession is permanent. And note the strange picture of a Nuer prophet (1956, facing p. 306) which shows the unkempt hair and beard 'both of which are objectionable to ordinary Nuer'. Their prophets stand outside the structuring of normal Nuer society. A prophet who is inspired by a spirit must give it a name

which distinguishes it as his particular spirit from the spirits of other prophets of his neighbourhood who are his rivals for renown and influence; for the attachment here is to individuals who built it up through a personal following and not, at least primarily, to social groups. (ibid.: 117)

To this extent they sustain my thesis that bodily control tends to be relaxed where social control is weak. The Nuer prophets look strange and unkempt; they operate outside the normal social structure, competing with one another for influence in a social dimension peculiar to themselves and distinct from the balanced opposition of lineage segments. By normal Nuer values, prophets have different moral standards. They are greedy, grasping and eccentric. They cure sickness caused by spirits and state their price in terms of cattle to be dedicated to spirits. Spirit-dedicated cattle represent transfers which restrict the flow of wealth through the secular channels of marriage payments and compensations. In fact, though individual prophets do well enough by their vocation, spirits are distinctly a nuisance to the general run of Nuer who would like their help but would also like them to stay away.

To sum up, using Ioan Lewis's terms, spirit possession is not part of the main morality cult of the Nuer but a peripheral cult. Whereas, among the Dinka, a benign form of spirit-possession lies at the centre of their religion and has none of these attributes.

Dinka spear-master clans and warrior clans are linked in descent and politics, the former specialized in ritual and the latter in political leadership, producing a balanced duality of power (Lienhardt, 1958: 118–19).

Leadership, in any Dinka political segment, necessarily involves the presence of two different classes or categories of clan, the warriors and the spear-masters, which are of equal and complementary status ... The Dinka masters of the fishing-spear are not merely ritual agents for composing feuds when the parties to them both wish it; they do not, as is usual for the Nuer leopard-skin chiefs, stand outside the structure of agnatic groups with which the political groups are identified in their relations with one another . . . (ibid.: 130–31)

Needless to say there is no question of spear-masters being shaggy, immoral, greedy, strange or grasping. They do not operate outside the social structure, but as a normal part of it.

As to their idea of spirit, Dinka in their rituals are much readier to expect good to come from abandoning themselves to it completely. Each clan has its own divinities, but the spear-master clans collectively recognize the divinity Flesh, the word which comes from the twitching of the flesh after a sacrificial beast is skinned which makes it appear to have a life of its own (1961: 136–7). The divinity Flesh is specially manifest in the quivering of legs and thighs at the onset of possession. The divinity Flesh ensures that the man who speaks by virtue of it speaks absolutely truthfully. Flesh means righteousness and justice. For my general comparison, it is worth noting that Dinka who are possessed by other, lesser divinities, become 'hysterically' possessed and are in a state of danger (1961: 57f. and 137), whereas the trembling of the spear-masters at sacrificial rites is always more controlled and safe. Thus the Dinka have two degrees of bodily uncontrol, associated appropriately with the centre and periphery of their religion, the centre and periphery of their social categories.

The Nuer attitude to possession is that it is dangerous in the first phase, and produces an abnormal, specialized role in the second phase; a role whose specialized task is to counteract the dangers of first phase possession. (The distinction between these phases has been developed by Ioan Lewis in a paper on witchcraft and spirit possession.) The Dinka attitude is that trance is the primary manifestation of unspecialized benign power. It is not restricted to a specialized role in the sense of calling for special initiation, by affliction, asceticism or training, but is open to all the adult males of a clan, and normally experienced by them all.

I believe I have summarized correctly a different religious bias in the two tribal cultures. By contrasting Nuer prophets with Dinka spear-masters I am able to emphasize a different value placed on bodily dissociation. The Nuer prophet has a special function in war, to compose hymns and rouse the fighting men. His role is not parallel to that of the Dinka spear-masters, whose clans are specialized for religion in juxtaposition with the warrior clans. The true parallel of the Dinka spear-master among the Nuer is the leopard-skin priest. In certain Nuer lineages a 'priestly virtue' is transmitted to their members (Evans-Pritchard, 1956: 292–3), which is an effective power to curse and bless and to perform sacrifice for certain occasions. Exactly the same word is used in each language to describe the source of this power, *ring*, which means flesh. It would seem that, at some stage in their development, the Nuer priestly lineages were also juxtaposed symmetrically with secular lineages in a similar pattern to the Dinka one (Evans-Pritchard, 1956: 293). Among the Dinka, Flesh is the chief divinity, whose cult we have described. It is a cult of physical dissociation and the attributes of flesh are etherialized into intellectual and moral qualities. Nuer priests invoke 'the spirit of our flesh . . . which refers to the spiritual source of sacerdotal power' (Evans-Pritchard, 1956: 109). Even if it were to transpire that the Nuer concept of flesh closely parallels the Dinka one, and this in spite of the many connotations of *ring*, flesh, with the physical as compared with other aspects of life (ibid.: 55, 154, 159), the much greater prominence and centrality of priestly possession as the channel of divine power for the Dinka would still distinguish theirs from Nuer religion. However great the difficulties of assessment, the question still remains that two neighbouring peoples, with two related languages, related histories and distinct political institutions, frequently at war with one another, have made different emphases in their use of the bodily mode.

The Nuer cosmos seems to be more rational and regulative. The connection they make between sickness and sin is so close that, though they believe in evil eye and in the work of fetishes and ghosts, they 'generally appear to feel that suffering is due to some fault of theirs' (1956: 21, 22 and 176). Moral faults, inherent in man's nature, tend to accumulate and predispose to disaster (ibid.: 193). Though they believe in luck, it does not intervene as an explanation of misfortune (ibid.: 195). The caprice element ranks low in their cosmological ideas. There are no inexplicable shocks or surprises in their universe. At death they mourn quietly, but not ostentatiously, since this might give the impression that God had not a perfect right to do whatever he wishes with them. Their general outlook on humankind and its fate is pessimistic. Though he writes about sacrifices to avert natural disasters, Evans-Pritchard says the Nuer are not very interested or hopeful about the efficacy of rites to change their fortune in hunting, agriculture or the seasons. 'Nuer rather turn their eyes inwards, to the little closed social world in which they live, they and their cattle. Their sacrifices are concerned with moral and spiritual, not natural crises' (ibid.: 200). Nuer are much more concerned than Dinka with automatic pollution. They recognize classes of offences which entail automatic misfortune. Incest is one such class; adultery, disrespect to in-laws and homicide are others. To each class of offence is imputed a particular class of illness. Incest produces skin disease; adultery afflicts the injured husband with pains in the lumbar region; and so on. A wider range of misfortunes may befall the man who uncovers his genitals in the presence of his in-laws or who drinks water after shedding human blood before purification. Most of the Nuer sacrifices are made to atone for one or other such offence, assumed to be the cause of illness (ibid.: VII). Here is an area of taboo-mindedness in Nuer religion which is at variance with their general disinclination for fetishes, charms and spells. But in these two areas of their life social constraints are strongly felt, marriage rules and local loyalty in fighting. Adultery, marriage and homicide are the main occasions for the transfer of cattle and the Nuer have less cattle than the Dinka. These transgressions held to be automatically dangerous express social relations in which Nuer most strongly feel the constraints of living in society.

By contrast, Dinka seem much less pollution-prone or taboo-minded. There is less emphasis in Lienhardt's book on Dinka religion on the piacular element in sacrifices. This could be a difference of focus in the observer. But I think not. Certainly the

Dinka seem to have a more optimistic world view. They do not expect their universe to be rational: 'The Dinka are in a universe which is largely beyond their control and where events may contradict the most reasonable human expectation' (Lienhardt, 1961: 54). They seem much less sin-conscious. An element of caprice is clearly linked with misfortune in their concept of the intriguing divinity, Macardit. He represents 'the final explanation of sufferings and misfortunes which cannot be traced to other causes more consonant with Dinka notions of Divinity as just . . . Macardit presides over the ending of good things, the inevitable and sometimes brutal curtailment of human life and fertility . . . a malign divinity specially associated with women' (1961: 81–3). So misfortune is not regularly traced to human faults. Is their notion of death less philosophical and passive than that of the Nuer? What does it signify that they cannot bear to speak of it, and bury their dead without looking at the grave as they shovel the earth in backwards? (Lienhardt, 1962). And what different quality of their beliefs leads them to bury their most famous spear-master alive so as to enact a kind of social triumph of life over death? (1961: 318). Sexual promiscuity is said to follow such a ceremony. Do the stricter Nuer have no such moments of licensed orgy in which marriage ties and incest rules are overridden? Or did their ethnographer just not happen to record them?

God, for the Nuer, is dangerous (Evans-Pritchard, 1956: 177, 195–6, 198). They are torn by a wish to keep him at a distance and have him near at hand to help them. The Dinka god, as we have seen, comes right down to possess intimately the bodies of his worshippers. He is not distant, evidently. Is he dangerous? I maintain that we are dealing here not with the different bias of two reporters who saw similar things differently. On the contrary, their close association gave them the same bias, as near as can be achieved by conscientious observation. The differences are precisely those we would predict from small differences in ecology and social structure summed up by Lienhardt in *Tribes without Rulers* (1958).

First, the Dinka are about four times more numerous than

Nuer; they live more densely. Then, most Dinka settlements straggle across savannah forest in continuous settlement; their sense of local bounded unit should be weaker than that of Nuer who live in discrete, wet season villages and concentrate in large cattle camps in the dry season. The pattern of Dinka transhumance has two phases of congregation, one in the dry season, their permanent settlements, the other in the height of the wet season. When 'flooding reduces the area available for grazing, such small groups (of cattle camps) are drawn together and converge on the few best sites in their neighbourhood. Toward the end of the rainy season, herdsmen of each tribe are concentrated in several sub-tribal camps' (1958: 100). Most significantly, Dinka speak of their political communities as cattle camps, and these 'are more fluid in composition and less fixed in their spatial relations to each other, than are permanent settlements ... Dinka country sets less rigid limits to movements in the wet season, and to the expansion of settlements, than are set by much of Nuer land for its people. These different ecological conditions are consistent with some differences between Nuer and Dinka political segmentation' (ibid.: 101). Lienhardt goes on to describe Dinka political theory which rests upon the assumption that groups expand, segment and break away from each other. 'Fission and fusion do not take place within a single genealogical framework' (ibid.: 104). Their political theory is one of expansion. In spite of the much higher density of population, it is a mobile social system in a sense in which the Nuer is not. 'They see their history as a spreading out and separation of peoples on the ground ... a notion which includes the notion of a measure of personal leadership' (ibid.: 118). The political framework is more confused and more fluid, genealogies are more muddled (ibid.: 106) than Nuer; lineages have fewer orders of formal segmentation. From this I conclude that it would be surprising if their categories for incest and bridewealth were as strict as those of the Nuer. Dinka recognize that they are capable of less wide-scale co-operation against common enemies than Nuer (ibid.: 108). These facts suggest that it is reasonable to place the Dinka further than Nuer along the diminishing lines of grid and group towards zero. If their idea of formal sin were alleged to be more highly developed than among the Nuer, it would be surprising, since these people are related in less inclusive and more easily evaded categories. I would not expect techniques of reconciliation and religious techniques of coercion to be so well developed. I would expect Nuer to be more magical and taboo-minded than the Dinka. The differences in their social structures, in the light of my hypothesis about symbolic behaviour, seem amply to justify the differences in the reporting of their religions. If it had been the other way, and the Dinka were reported to be more conscious of sin, more interested in purification, more afraid of the dangers of spirit possession, then the regular patterns apparent elsewhere would have suggested a subjective bias. But the more positive and more central use of bodily dissociation in Dinka religion turns out to be correlated with the predicted social variables.

To complete the demonstration, I would like to include another Nilotic tribe, the Mandari. On my reading of the ethnography they would appear on a diagram showing strength of grid and group as in Diagram 5.

Group, of course, refers to several possible levels of allegiance. The Mandari are acutely conscious of the widest one:

It is most important to bear in mind . . . that the small Mandari population in its tiny country is surrounded by powerful and numerous neighbours in vast territories and also that the Mandari population is itself made up of levels of immigrants dispersed around separated cores of original landowners, again of various kinds. (Buxton, 1963 and 1968: 49)

'Mandari country was composed of a very large number of small chiefdoms between whom relations were friendly, competitive or openly hostile' (1958: 71). So, at the level of small local chiefdom, group allegiance was important for Mandari. Within each chiefdom relations were stratified in a hierarchy which attributed ritual ties with the land to early groups of immigrants and validated their claims as landowners. The rights to political priority became matters of very tense competition,

Diagram 5: Three Nilotes

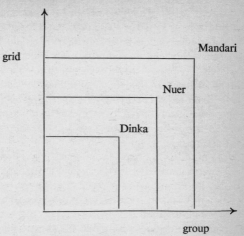

For the Mandari, grid and group are strongest; for the Nuer, they are weaker; for the Dinka, grid and group are weaker than for the Nuer.

as their attitude to clients as potential witches shows (Buxton, 1963). Restraints of grid and group seem to be highly charged emotional experiences. It is gratifying to find that their attitude to sin and to purification is very formalist. To the Mandari, sins, or pollutions, are specific acts; they are not made better or worse by the intentions of the sinner. Jean Buxton died suddenly in 1971. I had earlier spoken to her about this subject and she generally confirmed my impression of the greater magicality in the bias of Mandari culture. I recall a lively account she gave in a seminar in University College London of the complex colour and thermal categories into which Mandari class kinds of sins and kinds of illnesses. They prescribe sacrificial beasts with appropriate sex and markings for the purification of each kind of offence. But the pernickertiness of their rules drives them to desperate ritual shifts for transforming incorrectly 'hot' beasts, red ones or male ones, into the prescribed 'cool', white, black

129

or female forms. Their highly magical, formal approach to sin is in conformity with their attitude to spirit possession which seems closely to correspond to that which I have outlined for the Nuer. Possession is dangerous, causes sickness in the first phase and produces specialists in the second phase who are adept at countering the dangers they have themselves survived (1968: 40). She describes an 'elaborate specialist treatment' for a person whose sickness has been caused by a *nyok*, the vengeful spirit of a dead dog.

> The *nyok* screams 'Ahrrr! Ahrrrr!' and the doctor wrestles with it over the hole. He sways to and fro hanging on to the spear, while the spectators hold on to him; he foams at the mouth or blood pours from his nostrils. The *nyok* is said eventually to weaken and then to cease its struggles ... Treatment is in line with other exorcisms, and with convulsion therapy, where possession is induced by rhythmic rattle shaking. (ibid. : 60)

Thus I have compared three Nilotic peoples on the basis of grid and group. The material is very suggestive. I am tempted to find that their religious behaviour upholds the hypothesis. The weaker the social constraints, the more bodily dissociation is approved and treated as a central ritual adjunct for channelling benign power to the community. The stronger the social pressures, the more magicality in ritual and in the definition of sin.

It is important to notice two aspects of the Nuer-Dinka comparison which will be relevant to any wider discussion. First, the control of grid and group is not a function of population density. The Dinka in question live at a density of up to 60 to the square mile, the Nuer at roughly seven. Grid and group are a function of order and constraint in social relations and these can be as easily absent in dense as in sparse populations. The Dinka seem to think that they can break off social relations and start afresh quite easily. Their sense of living in an expanding economy may possibly be derived from their successful cattle husbandry. It makes a great difference to the quality of social life if people are sharing resources which seem to be expanding, dwindling or static. Paul Spencer has drawn attention to this variable in his comparison of Rendille and Samburu pastoralists in Kenya (1965: 293). He relates the much stricter social controls operating in Rendille society to the fact that Rendille 'believe that their camel herds, if they are growing at all, are growing at a *slower* pace than the human population' while 'the Samburu believe that their own cattle herds increase at a faster rate than their human population' and that the poorest of men may build up substantial herds. If the Nuer believe themselves to be husbanding a static livestock population and the Dinka an expanding one, this would be another explanation for why the latter take social control more lightly. Economic expansion and restriction turn out to be much more significant variables affecting cosmology than absolute population density as such.

I would not wish to brush off as unimportant the difficulties of interpretation which beset this argument. Any kind of illustrative material is intensely difficult to find for exactly the same reasons: no reports are exhaustive; none can avoid bias; there is an enormous subjective element of selection in any ethnographic observation. My particular kind of hypothesis depends on very close, objective assessment for its validation. Nothing will do but research which has been specially designed, not to prove it, but to test it.

Reviewing the shift from formal rite to positive approval of trance, I have referred here and there to co-varying ideas about sin. These should now be made more explicit. Along the series from maximum formality and control in symbolic behaviour to maximum informality and uncontrol there is a corresponding series in attitudes to wrong-doing. At the pole of maximum formality, the idea of wrong-doing takes no account of internal motive, or of the state of mind of the actor. Wrong-doing is bad in itself, its dangers are automatically unleashed, blame falls automatically, and the wrong is known *ex opere operato*. It exactly parallels the attitude to ritual in the case of extreme magicality. At the pole of maximum informality the idea of wrong-doing is entirely concerned with internal states of mind. The actual consequences of the act are of less concern than the wishes and intentions of the actor. Responsibility ends with

131

securing right motives. To take homicide as an example, at one end of the range we have automatic pollution of blood, at the other unintended manslaughter distinguished from homicide. I would expect these variations to coincide smoothly with variations in formality and informality and both in accordance with the hold of grid and group on individuals in relevant contexts. Thus I would expect to find whole cultures where ideas of sin are more internal, less taboo-ridden than the ideas of their close neighbours, who experience more effective and all-embracing social constraints.

To show how this can be examined, let me break my methodological strictures and dare to compare widely separated peoples. The comparison of the pygmies with Hadza hunters in Tanzania is so illuminating in this matter of sin that I must discuss them together. I have earlier described the fluidity of the Mbuti pygmy camps. Their groupings are so undefined, so unimportant in their lives that no tribe in Africa seems to emphasize group membership less than they, with the exception of the Hadza. The latter move even more freely in and out of camp, forming new ones and moving away. The description of camp groupings poses a serious problem of method for their ethnographer (J. C. Woodburn, 1964). We would expect then that they would have internalized the idea of sin even more completely than the pygmies. But this is not so. The Mbuti pygmies have no conception of pollution, neither pollution of death, nor of birth, nor of menstruation. But the Hadza fear pollution of menstrual blood. To interpret this taboo, I need to leave the question of group and return to grid. The pygmies are as free of social categories as they are of bounded groups. Neither sex, age, nor kinship order their behaviour in strictly ordained categories. Turnbull writes:

It would, of course, be ridiculous to deny that there is any system of kinship, but it is certain that the kinship system does not have the same importance as a focal point of social control as it may have in other African societies. To my mind this is undeniably linked to the *ad hoc* nature of the society, with its almost complete lack of concern for the past, as for the future ... The effective kinship terminology at once reflects the situation, which only becomes confused when any attempt is made to relate the terms to their usage in village society. It distinguishes generations rather than kin and cuts indiscriminately across actual kinship boundaries . . . (1965 : 109–10)

So also with sex, they place little emphasis on separate male and female spheres. Men and women share in tasks of erecting huts and even in hunting. Social categories are markedly weak. It is the young men who operate the system of social control on behalf of the camp.

This is perfectly compatible with their general lack of concern for sin. In this kind of culture people would readily believe Mary Kingsley's missionaries who taught that 'a little talk with Jesus makes it all alright'. Informality is the key-note of their religious practice. I have not counted how often the words 'intimacy' and 'joy' occur in Turnbull's account, but they are very frequent.

Even more leaderless and free in movement from camp to camp and spouse to spouse, the Hadza are divided by a social category so dominating and all-inclusive that Woodburn is tempted to describe it as a quasi-group. Wherever Hadza are, and whatever they do, they are always controlled by the division between the sexes. This division is between two hostile classes, each of which is capable of organizing itself for defence or virulent attack against the other. This extraordinarily intense consciousness of sexual difference is the only permanent level of organization the Hadza ever achieve. It is the background of male competition for wives, of female collusion between mothers and daughters to exact the maximum of trade goods from husbands in return for grudgingly given sexual satisfaction. The very low level of the division of labour between the sexes is itself an added difficulty in the way of building up a set of long-term conjugal relations. Keep in mind the insecurity of a man's hold on his wife, and their belief in menstrual pollution appears to have a practical value. When a Hadza woman menstruates, she must avoid certain activities which would be polluted by her contact. But not only must she rest. Her husband of the moment, whoever he may be, must himself abstain from manly activities lest he endanger the rest of the camp's chance of success in hunting. So his menstrual couvade is a kind of claim he affirms regularly by asserting the physiological connection between himself and his wife and the wide-spread dangers of disregarding it (Woodburn, op. cit.: 204–78; Douglas, 1968c).

Here we find, amid a general lack of concern for purity and danger, a strong regard for certain specific, symbolic boundaries. A symbolic expression of the tie between husband and wife (sanctioned by the threat of danger to the whole camp) reflects the one relationship which is highly valued. It expresses the one social category which is an active regulator of behaviour, the distinction of men and women, and it draws the boundary between the sexes in such a way as to incorporate the husband, in the restricted context of his conjugal claims, within the same line which encompasses his wife. So the rule, which in its general form sets all women apart from all men and treats them as dangerous, in its particular incidence sets each woman apart from other women, but not apart from her husband; he, in his turn, is, in virtue of his married state, set apart from other men. Thus the pollution rule draws very precise lines of incorporation and exclusion. No jump of the imagination is required to see this formal taboo, in an otherwise taboo-free system, as expressing the pressure of social relations. Thus I take it as a starting point for demonstrating the hypothesis that when social relations are not finely ascribed, when they are easily broken off and carry little in the way of obligation or privilege, the formal aspect of wrong-doing is disregarded. The more fluid and formless are social relations, the more internalized the idea of wrong-doing. The full demonstration requires, as I insisted earlier, the social and symbolic behaviour of the Haḏza to be compared from this angle with their close neighbours and similarly for the pygmies. But until the interest of such an examination has been suggested, the work of analysis will not be carried out.

These examples throw considerable light on present theological attitudes to the subject of sin. What is taken to be a more advanced, enlightened doctrine appears merely as the usual expression of a less differentiated experience of social relations.

We have here a glimpse of the sociological matrix in which ideas about sin and the self are generated. No simple evolutionary pattern emerges. It is not a history of the victory of liberal tolerance over bigoted intolerance. The relation of self to society varies with the constraints of grid and group: the stronger these are, the more developed the idea of formal transgression and its dangerous consequences, and the less regard is felt for the right of the inner self to be freely expressed. The more that social relations are differentiated by grid and group, the more the private individual is exhorted to pour his passions into prescribed channels or to control them altogether. In the small-scale primitive social system (whether we identify with high classification or with small group) a continual feedback process modifies the public pattern of roles so that no great discrepancy can arise. How the private individual sees his interests and how society at large expects him to respond will more or less coincide. All the pressures upon him are personal pressures. He is as capable of modifying them by his action as they are of controlling him. The great difference between us, in modern industrial society, and them, in small-scale primitive society, is that the feedback is lost. The pressures exerted on the individual are not modified by his reaction. There is no arguing with or explaining to the industrial system any more than there is arguing with the weather. The strongest social controls are not exerted in the personal mode.

We find ourselves generally with the other primitive societies I have identified with strong grid. They share with us the paradox that the sense of sin is weakened as social control is strengthened. Just as society demands more and more urgently that our passions flow in the channels it prescribes, we are more and more deaf to its inducements. Because of the disjunction between its classifications and our aims we hear the more insistent demand of the inner self to be given full expression.

7 The Problem of Evil

Pain and injustice do not pose problems, social or religious, for everyone. Indeed, in any part of society located to the left of the vertical line, they attract scant reflection. To the right, where social control is strong, I will argue from three types of social experience that the problem of evil is posed in characteristically different ways. We are now approaching the crux of the comparison with Bernstein's analysis of family control systems. For each type of family there is its necessary manner of validating coercive demands. For each distinct type of social environment, likewise, there is its necessary manner of justifying coercion. Through the classifications used, the furniture of the universe is turned into an armoury of control. In each social system human suffering is explained in a way that reinforces the controls. To see how evil is understood, we must see classification and personal pressure, grid and group, working together.

In the first place, we can quickly dispose of high classification, strong grid and group. These people use the incidence of misfortune to uphold the moral law. Disease and accident are either attributed to moral failures or invested with nobility in a general metaphysical scheme which embraces suffering as part of the order of being. There is no lack of ethnography to illustrate this classic form of the problem.

Moving down towards zero we come to the small groups exerting strong personal pressures, but with weak classification. Here flourishes a theory of evil that generally corresponds to fear of witchcraft. This is a cosmos dominated by ill-will and jealousy. Jane Austen made Emma smugly remark: 'A very narrow income has a tendency to contract the mind, and sour the temper. Those who can barely live and who live perforce in a very small and generally very inferior society may well be illiberal and cross.' It is not poverty in itself, but the contraction and above all the confusion of social ties which go with the witchcraft syndrome. Small competitive communities tend to believe themselves in a dangerous universe, threatened by sinister powers operated by fellow human beings. Instead of prayer, fasting and sacrifice to the deity, ritual activity is devoted to witch hunting, witch-cleansing, witch-killing and curing from the effects of witchcraft.

The anthropological model for this type comes from Central Africa where the studies of Marwick (1952, 1965) and Mitchell (1956) and others following them have defined a type of witchcraft situation. It is one in which accusations of witchcraft are used to denigrate rivals and pull them down in the competition for leadership. The accusations would not have this effect if roles were clearly defined and rules of succession unambiguous. But it is the essence of this situation that men can entertain contradictory views of their roles. The elder brother is supposed to be benevolent and authoritative, but his ability to sustain the role convincingly is undermined by the knowledge that each and all of his younger brothers is his rival in the succession to the headmanship of the village. Ambiguity allows competition within a closed circle of kin and neighbours. In the competition the dangerous powers of the universe are alleged to be under the control of the rival, to whose door all succeeding misfortunes are laid. Here failure is not ascribed to bad luck, nor to moral failings of the victim, but to the hostile, occult powers of his neighbour. Eventually the witch, whom rumour tries at the bar of public opinion, must either allow the village to split or clear his name in some ordeal. The work of Central Africanists enables us to specify precisely the social structure conducive to this particular type of witch-cosmology. But it is not by any means a Central African phenomenon. In Central America, among the Trio and Shevante, Peter Rivière can make a similar analysis. Witchcraft accusations are either used to expel an unwanted member of the community, or to split the village into two parts, each part supposing itself to have thus sloughed off its dangerous elements (1970).

If this is the social structure in which witch beliefs flourish, we should expect to find something approximating to witchcraft wherever these conditions prevail. In short, if we have social units whose external boundaries are clearly marked, whose internal relations are confused, and which persist on a small scale, then we should look for the active witchcraft type of cosmology. Somehow we must bring the association with cats and broomsticks under control by eliciting some general characteristics of these beliefs. First, to accuse of witchcraft is to accuse of evil practice on a cosmic scale. The witch is no ordinary thief or adulterer, or even a common traitor. He is accused of a perverted nature, or of alliance with the enemies of human kind, in Europe with the devil, in other continents with carnivorous predators. He is associated symbolically with the reverse of the way that a normal human lives, with night instead of day. His powers are abnormal, he can fly, be in two places at once, change his shape. Above all, he is a deceiver, someone whose external appearance does not automatically betray his interior nature. Very common all over the world is some idea equivalent to the witches' coven. Though each coming from different social groups, the witch sinks his local loyalties in favour of obligations to his confraternity. In the end, if he fails to satisfy them, they will devour him.

If we take these beliefs about the nature of the witch to signify something about the nature of the society which takes them seriously, we are struck by a close portrayal of the witch-believing social system. For here, as we saw, the body politic tends to have a clear external boundary, and a confused internal state in which envy and favouritism flourish and continually confound the proper expectations of members. So the body of the witch, normal-seeming and apparently carrying the normal human limitations, is equipped with hidden and extraordinarily malevolent powers. The loyalty of the witch, instead of being committed firmly to his group, flies out loose. He goes alone to contend with alien personifications of lust and power. The witch himself has no firm anchorage in the social structure. In appearance he is present, but only bodily; his real inner self has escaped from social restraint.

A closer look at the symbolism of witchcraft shows the dominance of symbols of inside and outside. The witch himself is someone whose inside is corrupt; he works harm on his victims by attacking their pure, innocent insides. Sometimes he sucks out their soul and leaves them with empty husks, sometimes he poisons their food, sometimes he throws darts which pierce their bodies. And then again, sometimes he needs access to their inner bodily juices, faeces, semen, spittle, before he can hurt them. Often such bodily excretions are the weapons of his craft. If we were to make an analysis of the symbols of attack, I predict we would find a close correspondence between the experience of the social system and the kind of attack most feared. Soul sucking and poisoning we would expect to be practised by the witch within the local community, weapon throwing by the far-off witch.

So much for the cosmic scale on which the witch characteristically is conceived. To imagine a witch it is necessary to reflect on human nature, to consider its limitations in space and time and to believe in its natural proclivity to justice and goodness; the witch is the converse of a normal human. Now for the social uses of the belief. In these small and simple social structures, with very little differentiation of roles, techniques for distancing, regulating, and reconciling are little developed. The witch doctrine is used as the idiom of control, since it pins blame for misfortune on trouble-makers and deviants. The accusation is a righteous demand for conformity. In a community in which overt conflict cannot be contained, witchcraft fears are used to justify expulsion and fission. These are communities in which authority has very weak resources. Beyond a certain size, they cannot persist without introducing sharper definition into the structure of roles. Only certain limited targets can be achieved by their low level of organization. Expulsion of dissidents is one method of control, fission of the group a more drastic one. In either case the group remains small and disorganized. The doctrine of a cosmos inhabited by normal humans and by witches disguised as humans is well adapted to the dynamics of renewal and continuity in such social systems.

There are thus four general characteristics of the witchcraft cosmology: the idea of the bad outside and the good inside, the inside under attack and in need of protection, human wickedness on a cosmic scale, and these ideas used in political manipulation. The symbols of black cats and broomsticks are local expressions of this complex of beliefs which, once identified in general terms, can be found more widely – I would even dare to suggest it may be found wherever the social preconditions exist.

Let me take an English sectarian movement, from the history of the Exclusive Brethren, as an example.

No apology is needed for moving from African witchcraft to English sects. Bryan Wilson himself has blazed the trail in his valuable set of studies of sectarianism (1967). He concludes his discussion of the Exclusive Brethren with just such a comparison:

> It might be said of the Brethren, that there is an elaborated Durkheimian point to be made, that – in a sense not far removed from that in which the idea was developed for a tribal people – their worship of God is worship of the community. The worship is more elaborate; the relationships are more consciously recognized; and yet the assembly appears as a form of the Deity ... The community, the assembly – has a sense of special sanctity from which individual and household sanctity is derived; it employs severe measures of 'social hygiene' for its maintenance. (Wilson, 1967: 336)

These measures are equivalent to witch hunting and witch expulsion. The Exclusive Brethren, which Wilson classifies as an 'Introversionist Sect', remain true to their principles of rejecting human organization. Thus they deviate from the common trend for sects to evolve into denominations in the course of two generations. They have not grown and diversified, they have remained aloof from secular society for over 100 years. The price they have paid for maintaining themselves as a pure group is the erecting of a high wall between themselves and the rest of the world, and continual schism. As in witch-dominated systems, doctrine is used as a weapon of expulsion and separation. As in witch beliefs, the doctrine celebrates the purity and goodness of one part of mankind, and the vileness of the rest.

The idea of the saints already inhabiting heavenly places; the dissociation of the saints from Israel; and their different prospects from those of the world – are conceptions reinforced in their separatist consequences by teachings concerning the will of Christ and the will of man. Christ's expression 'Not my will, but thine be done' is regarded as a form of assertion that there never was any divergence between the Father's will and the Son's. Nor should there be any divergent will in man, since all free will is seen as 'self will'. Man's only will is the will to sin. In contrast, the saints must act under the direction of the Holy Spirit, and this reasserts the authority of the fellowship over the individual, and encourages quietism towards the outside world. (ibid.: 285)

The Brethren aver that they have love to all the saints but that this can only be actually shown to those in the Fellowship. Yet, although theoretically the Brethren acknowledge the possibility of saints existing outside the Fellowship, they have sometimes behaved as if this were an entirely theoretical circumstance. The growth of emphasis on ecclesiological rectitude, the frequency of excommunication and the development of a more exacting ethic, have all occurred on the latent assumption that the fellowship was the only manifestation of the Church. Thus, during the 1860s a system was developed in which the Park Street assembly, which was Darby's assembly, brought heresy that occurred elsewhere virtually to the test of London judgement. London expelled in this period a Mr Stewart. The Walworth assembly enquired about the grounds of the expulsion, and on enquiry were not entirely satisfied. Subsequently, they moved their meeting to Peckham. London responded by excluding Peckham from their communion, which meant virtual excommunication of all in the assembly. Soon afterwards, a Mr Goodall of Peckham visited Sheffield and was received by the saints there at table. On this becoming known, Sheffield was also excommunicated by London, in deference to the long-established principle of eliminating all taint. On being questioned, Darby referred to the Church of God on earth, and said, 'being outside . . . of what it represents in London . . . is to be outside it altogether'. (ibid.: 294)

It is very tempting to work through this admirable book and to make an analysis of the relation of the various sects to the outside society in the terms of this discussion, that is of the influence of grid and group on their doctrines. Most of them started, in what Wilson calls the pre-sectarian stage, by shunning all forms of social organization. Those which succeeded in maintaining for any length of time this total rejection of authority and formality, usually paid for it the price of doctrinal nullity. They stood together and welcomed all comers, but stood for nothing. Those who felt after some such experience the need for some doctrinal content would tend to draw in their ranks, close their boundaries and set themselves in the direction of sectarianism and schism. Those who steered a middle course, who tried to convert the world to their doctrines and developed an organization for the purpose, gradually lost the singularity of their message, for the latter would seem to be vital only so long as it expresses a certain low level of undifferentiated social relations. In this way, the Plymouth Brethren started in 1829 seeking to unite all true believers in a biblical fellowship, reacting against institutionalism and ecclesiology:

> Communion was the bond of common life which brought into unity those who might not always agree on doctrinal matters or procedures of worship, but who accepted an informal non-hierarchic lay assembly of those who took their stand on the Scriptures. Their principle was fellowship in the Spirit, participation in a common life, although with freedom to visit other religious assemblies and even to worship with groups of rather different doctrinal persuasions. (ibid.: 244)

Here we have described exactly the social structure specified for the witchcraft cosmology. The sect is founded on a particular idea of human nature, emphasizing fellowship and goodwill, and shunning principles of organization. Expulsions are used as the method of control which enables the group to go on believing in the possibility of living united in the spirit, but without hierarchy and formality. When we look more closely at the cosmology, we find the predicted principles. The inside is so good that within the Fellowship they are all saints; the outside is bad. Not only is there the alleged corruption of those who happen not to be within the Fellowship, but there is also the general badness of institutionalized behaviour, of seeking to relate Churches to the civil power, to take over the work of the spirit by establishing external forms. The contrast of the spirit with flesh, of spontaneity and freedom with instituted form, the contrast of thing signified with sign, is equated in the doctrinal controversies with the contrast of God with man. So the significance of inside-outside takes on cosmic proportions and the heretic is the saint who wants to have some truck with the outside.

These aspects of sectarianism emerge clearly in the life of John Nelson Darby, whose appearance has been described in Chapter 5. His life was an endless struggle with dissidents on this very score. They felt that to insure continuity his standard suggestions were inadequate. In the pamphlet entitled *Reflections on the Ruined Condition of the Church and on the Efforts Making* (sic) *by Churchmen and Dissenters to Restore It to its Primitive Order* (1841) he wrote:

> . . . the project of making Churches is really the hindrance in the way of the accomplishment of what all desire, namely the union of the saints in one body – first, because those who have attempted it, having gone beyond the power given them by the Spirit, the flesh has been fostered in them. (Coad, 1968: 125)

The biographer goes on to say

> Darby concluded his pamphlet with his standard suggestions, which were so inadequate for continuing congregations. The present dispensation was fallen, and any who tried to remedy this state had failed to grasp the Divine Will. The promise of the presence of Christ when two or three were present in his name was still valid. Christians should avail themselves of this promise, and so meet to wait upon God, but no more. There was promise and power for such meetings, but none at all for those who sought to set up churches. To choose presidents or pastors is to organize a church, and even the appointment of elders is now impossible. The only government of the church was the acknowledgement of the Spirit of God. (ibid.: 127)

Not only was error wrong, but for Darby 'error was something evil, directly involving the honour of the Godhead' (ibid.: 87). So in his controversy with a former friend and disciple, associating heresy with evil and with the devil, he wrote:

My mind did pass through the same process of anxiety as that of which you speak, as far as anxiety went, a qualm crossed my mind that some work of the enemy more than I knew how to judge of, was at the bottom. (ibid.: 143)

The cosmic implications of God and the devil; inside and outside; purity within, corruption without; here is the complex of ideas that is associated with small groups with clearly marked membership and confusion of internal roles. The fact that I have drawn on Darby's own attitudes raises the question of his personality. It is a distraction to this discussion to suggest that persecution feelings and a capacity to identify one's own views with those of the Almighty, and so to magnify the personal conflicts to a cosmic scale, are psychopathic manifestations. So they may be and Darby may well have had these tendencies to an abnormal degree. So also, possibly, many of his followers. But we cannot regard the psychological explanation as satisfactory by itself without ignoring the correlation of social structure with cosmology. Anyone who has had the experience of a free and open social context changing to a suddenly restricted one in which ascribed relationships have not been worked out must recognize the change in attitudes of all the persons affected by the contraction and confusion of social ties. Leaders may well have psychological traits which enable them to express very sharply these fears and resentments, but only a sociological analysis can explain why they find their followings in predictable niches whose social structure corresponds recognizably with the dominant pattern of symbols.

We have signalled a similarity in philosophical outlook common to small bounded communities. It can be described as a form of metaphysical dualism. For its doctrine of two kinds of humanity, one good, the other bad, and the association of the badness of some humans with cosmic powers of evil is basically similar to some of the so-called dualist religions which are discussed by historians. If indeed we can relate philosophical dualism to certain kinds of social structures, then some re-examination of the history of ideas is called for. No longer should it be permitted for historians to write as if philosophies move autonomously in a social vacuum, one idea hitting another, splitting it, growing, decaying and being taken over. Why did Zoroaster rebel against polytheism? Why did he think that a good God could not be responsible for evil? Or, to put it more cogently, why was there a following for a man who could not tolerate the idea of a punishing God, but split the universe between two equally balanced warring deities, one good, one bad? It takes a certain kind of social experience to start to worry about the problem of evil. Not everyone can perceive it as a problem at all. The question of God's responsibility does not pose itself in the terms which historians customarily employ:

It is only when one has come to admit one omnipotent, omniscient creator, who created the world with all there is in it, that the question arises why everything in the world does not go according to the will of the creator and ruler ... in other words, the question arises as to how evil came into the world. An attempt to answer this question; such is dualism in its different forms ... The whole history of Western Philosophy appears in this light as an alternation of dualism and monism since Aristotle was already combating Plato's dualism and since his own monism, with that of the Stoics, was succeeded by a period of pagan and christian neo-Platonism up to the Aristotelian revival in the twelfth century. Plato himself did not invent dualism *ex stirpe*, for it was foreshadowed by Empedocles, Anaxagoras, the Orphics and Pythagoreans. (Duchesne-Guillemin, 1958: 1, 71–2)

The mind of the anthropologist boggles at the erudition required to apply sociological insights to the problem of evil in such a perspective. For certainly dualism through these centuries took varying forms, some emphasizing more the contrast between spirit and matter, some emphasizing more the human agents of evil, others emphasizing demons. With each, we would expect appropriately varying social conditions.

The Pentecostal Church of West Indians in London which I have mentioned already would 'disfellowship' a member who unsuccessfully challenged the leader. The man thus expelled would often go off and form a new church around his own leadership. The charges made against him, usually of sexual irregularity, may have had implications of a more deep-dyed and sinister form of villainy in the eyes of the Fellowship than in ours. But this does not appear from Calley's account. I would hardly expect to find the witchcraft cosmology established in a community whose boundaries are so fluctuating and memberships so fluid. A close analysis of sectarian movements on the criteria of grid and group should reveal such consistently varying patterns of cosmology and social structure.

The only way in which a witch-dominated cosmology can be transformed is by a change at the level of social organization. John Middleton has described a cyclic move between ascribed and competitive social patterns with the predicted shift in cosmological emphasis (Middleton, 1960). In the early stages of the growth of a new Lugbara lineage, leadership is ascribed by seniority in the male line. At this stage, though witch beliefs are latent, they seem to lie inactive. All fortunes, good and bad, are sent by punishing ancestors who regulate behaviour through the mediation of the lineage elder. But as the lineage grows in size and as the elder ages and weakens, problems of succession split the group into rival factions. Competition replaces ascription. The ancestors recede into the background while accusations of witchcraft are bandied about by rivals for the leadership. Once the succession problem is settled (by the death or disgrace of the declining elder) ascription and the ancestors take over again.

People who frequently accuse one another of witchcraft readily adopt witch-cleansing movements. In central Africa these movements spread like wildfire from tribe to tribe where small self-contained villages are dominated by witch beliefs. These movements offer fantastic promises of a new golden age to be realized on earth by the ending of witchcraft. But it is important to note that witch-cleansing movements are not the same as millennial movements properly so-called. Witch-cleansing movements, though they spread from one community to the next, spread as solutions offered to a given community and its members for their particular troubles. They are not formulae for saving the world in general, or the whole tribe. Their exponents go round from village to village like a decontamination squad selling techniques for de-fusing potentially explosive human material. When they have made their rounds, the community sees itself restored (albeit temporarily) to a state of tranquil harmony. For so long as the spell lasts all suspected witches are rendered harmless and the witchcraft is under control; livestock will fatten, crops will flourish, children will grow strong and no one die till a ripe old age. Symbolism of the bounded social group is very clear in the witch-cleansing movement (Douglas, 1963; Richards, 1935; Marwick, 1950). The perfection of the body and the completion of life's span are promised through the control of witchcraft, which is the only perceived threat to the unity of the group. The witch-cleansing movement staves off schism and shores up the weak internal organization of the group. But eventually a child sickens, crops fail and strife breaks out again. The cult is said to have lost its force.

Although the witch-cleansing movement carries a millennial possibility in its promise to end evil and suffering, it differs radically from the true millennial movement. It is focused on the problems of small local groups, whereas millennialism has a message for the world. But like the millennial movement, the witch-cleansing movement comes and goes and leaves the community as it was, still prone to witch beliefs, still awaiting a new, more effective movement which will kill off or immobilize witches for ever. Neither can succeed in separating the social structure permanently from its appropriate cosmology.

The witch-fearing cosmology goes with a closely bounded unit. When association is free and escape from unwanted ties easy, the question of evil does not take this particular form. Witch-dominated cosmologies are rare among nomadic hunters and herders.

Pastoralists who neighbour the Nuer, the Dinka, believe in witchcraft as a possibility. They are able to indicate the physical abnormalities which betray a witch, but they very rarely accuse of witchcraft (Lienhardt, 1951). Navaho sheepherders in Arizona, of whom we wrote in the first chapter, believe in witchcraft. 'Out of a Navaho group of 500 members, nineteen living individuals have been accused (in gossip – not publicly) of witchcraft. Ten additional individuals who have been dead from ten to thirty years have been so accused. In the last thirty years there have been six public accusations – "trials" – and two "witches" have been killed' (Kluckhohn, 1944: 58). It took Kluckhohn years of work to obtain more than anecdotal reference to witches 'over the mountain' or 'across the reservation' but none the less it was an important concern of these Navaho who spent most of the year in small family groups pent up together but isolated from others. On the other hand, those Navaho observed by Aberle later, who had suffered from de-stocking and the cash economy and taken comfort in the peyote cult, had lost interest in witchcraft (Aberle, 1966: 203–4). By and large witchcraft beliefs are likely to flourish in small enclosed groups, where movement in and out is restricted, when interaction is unavoidably close, and where roles are undefined or so defined that they are impossible to perform. Strindberg shrewdly describes a society of this kind in the home of his own childhood. The society of urban Sweden in the 1850s was divided into classes, or rather natural divisions according to trade and occupation, which held each other in check:

The child's first impressions, as he remembered afterwards, were of fear and hunger. He was afraid of the dark, of spankings, of upsetting everybody. Afraid of falling, of hurting himself, of being in the way. He was afraid of being hit by his brothers, slapped by the maids, scolded by his grandmother, caned by his father, and birched by his mother . . . Above the child loomed a hierarchy of authorities wielding various rights and powers, ranging from the seniority privileges of his brothers to the supreme tribunal of his father. And yet above his father was the 'super' who always threatened him with the landlord . . . But even above him was the general . . . The child did not know what a king looked like, but he knew that the general went up to the King . . . When his mother prayed to God in the evening, the child could form no distinct idea of Him, except that he must certainly be higher than the King. (Strindberg, 1967: 18–19)

Here is a perfect description of a distant God to whom the child automatically relates through the clearly felt layers of social hierarchy. He then describes the confusion and troubles which beset the family – and the sense of crowding.

Three rooms were occupied by the father and mother with their seven children and two servants. The furniture consisted mostly of tables and beds. Children on ironing boards and chairs, children in cradles and beds. The father had no room for himself, although he was at home most of the time . . . The family was and still is a very imperfect institution. No one had time to bring up the children. The school took over where the maids left off. The family was really an institution for eating, washing and ironing, and a very uneconomical one at that. Nothing but cooking, shopping, running errands to the greengrocer and dairy. Washing, ironing, starching and scouring. Too many things for such a small number of persons to do at once . . . The child heard only that he had duties, not that he had rights. Everyone else's wishes were listened to; his were ignored. He could do nothing without doing something wrong, go nowhere without being in someone's way, utter no word without disturbing someone. Finally he did not even dare move. The supreme duty and greatest virtue was to sit on a chair and be quiet. (ibid.: 30–32)

This gives us an unbeatable account of roles being impossibly defined so as to produce frustration and, in the long run, ambiguity and confusion. Strindberg, as a sensitive child,

was in perpetual anxiety lest he should do something wrong. But he was always on the alert for injustice, and by setting a high standard for himself, he carefully watched the failings of his brothers. When they went unpunished, he felt deeply wronged; when they were undeservedly rewarded, his sense of justice suffered. With the result that he was considered envious. (ibid.: 32–3)

One older brother was his father's favourite, the other his mother's. He was no one's favourite. Then he goes on to describe the frequent miscarriage of justice from which he suffered and which, as it accumulated, type-cast him in the family as secretive, jealous and cold. His whole description of the social setting and the response of members of the group parallels situations which give rise to witchcraft beliefs with uncanny exactness. And of course it is August Strindberg, the child who was nobody's favourite, who is accused of an abnormal, defective personality.

To live in this kind of society is to live crowded together with one's fellow humans in disorderly competition. Its members have reason to lack confidence that justice will prevail. Not theirs the motto about the mills of God grinding slowly but grinding exceedingly small. In the life of pastoralists such as Dinka and Nuer the great imponderables are hazards of climate and pasture; fellow humans are fairly reliable. In this other kind of society the hazards and frustrations are produced by fellow humans.

This contrast is made very clearly by Godfrey Lienhardt, when he compares the Nuer and Dinka with another Nilotic people, the Anuak (1962). As he put it:

> The Anuak are basically agricultural and sedentary, living in many distinct, largely self-sufficient and often very crowded village communities, where they are in constant and intense individual contact. The Dinka–Nuer are first and foremost pastoral people necessarily transhumant, with regular dispersal and regrouping of members of local communities. In the nature of their occupation, the Dinka–Nuer individually live more solitary lives than the Anuak.
> The frequent dispersal of the Dinka–Nuer as compared with the concentration of the Anuak may be associated with a much greater interest shown by the Anuak in individuals and personalities. They have an extensive psychological vocabulary, and their village politics . . . are conducted through an interplay of character as well as of faction. Anuak are interested in people, Dinka–Nuer more interested in cattle. For the Anuak their lively interest is a practical necessity in the conduct of their village affairs with their frequent plots for the promotion of sectional and individual interests in the headmanship. The competitive system of rank and influence permits any ambitious individual a wider scope for political activity . . . an Anuak who feels himself slighted by a particular headman will eventually find those with whom to combine in an attempt to replace him or he can go and seek favour at a noble's court. The Anuak have institutions based on favouritism and competitiveness for favour, which could not develop among the Nuer–Dinka, who have no individuals of rank whom it could be profitable to cultivate. (1962: 74–85)

We hardly need to fill in the cosmology of the Anuak. Whereas Dinka–Nuer believe misfortune and death to be sent by spirit powers which correspond to the social order, Anuak attribute deaths to witches or to ghostly vengeance of dead people whom their victims have somehow wronged in their life. Whereas the Nuer–Dinka respond to sickness by sacrifice and prayer 'the only religious expert among the Anuak is the Ajuan, a person – most usually a woman – whose main traditional tasks were to find witches and deal with witchcraft and to try to remove ghostly curses from its victim' (op. cit.: 85).

The choices people make about how they deal with one another are the real material which concerns the student of comparative religion. This is the missing dimension which must be added to psychoanalysis for its insights to illumine. Jung's comments on the Reformation, for instance, treat the impoverishment of symbols in European culture as the result of a dialectic of the mind:

The iconoclasm of the Reformation, however, quite literally made a breach in the bulwarks of the holy pictures and, ever since, one after another has crumbled away. They became dubious, for they collided with awakening reason ... The history of the development of Protestantism is one of chronic iconoclasm. One wall after another fell. And the work of destruction was not too difficult either, when once the authority of the church had been shattered. We all know how, in large things as in small, in general as well as in particular, piece after piece collapsed, and how the alarming impoverishment of symbolism that is now the condition of our life came about. (Jung, 1940: 60–61)

Do we know how it came about? In general we tend to accept implicitly with Jung that the movement is as inevitable as the growth of technology and even that it may have something to do with increase of knowledge in general, 'awakening reason', a kind of sad maturity and coming of age. As he says:

That the gods die from time to time is due to man's discovery that they do not mean anything, that they are good-for-nothings made by human hands, fashioned out of wood and stone. In reality, man has thus discovered only this: that up till then he had not achieved one thought concerning these images. (loc. cit.)

He then goes on to defend the rejection of symbols as an achievement in its own right, and to present it in terms of the good inside, spirit, being preferable to worthless outside, of content preferred above empty form.

... I am convinced that Protestant man has not in vain been despoiled of his own development, and made to go naked. This development has an interconsistency. Everything that presented him with no thought-content has been torn from him ... As the Christian vow of worldly poverty turned the senses from the good things of the world, so spiritual poverty seeks to renounce the false riches of the spirit. (ibid.: 63–4)

Jung would be the first to agree that the individual suffers no absolute impoverishment of his private symbolic life. The theory of archetypes and the analysis of dreams depends on this. Therefore the beggary to which he refers is the loss of coherence in publicly recognized symbolic structures. And this derives from the coherence of the social structures and declines with decline in that realm. Thus the glowing eulogy of spiritual poverty as a source of strength and self-knowledge for the individual becomes very dubious. First, because the scope of self-knowledge is reduced by restricted experience of other selves. Second, the fullest self-knowledge will take account of the social conditions which affect the development of the self. Third, it cannot be assumed that the point near zero, where pressures of grid and group are at a minimum, presents the ideal conditions for the development of the individual personality.

8   Impersonal Rules

Witch beliefs express a division within humanity: there are
pure, good men, and utterly vile men who do not belong with
humanity at all. We have argued that this dualism is fostered
by the experience of living in small, closed communities. We
now turn to societies where this experience is lacking. Where a
man is expected to build his own career by transacting with all
and sundry as widely as possible to the best of his ability, there
is a very different view of human nature. In these competitive
conditions, men are not set on either side of a line dividing
humanity from inhumanity. They are seen to be unequally
endowed with talents, but the inequality is random, unpredictable
and unconnected with moral judgement.

Two New Guinea tribes show slight variations on the theme.
First, the Garia of the Madang District on the north coast of New
Guinea. About 2500 of them inhabited 35 square miles of the
Bagasin Area. They lived in small hamlets consisting of dwellings
grouped around a cult house. Notice how the ties of common
residence are not congruent with those of personal allegiance.
Lawrence (1964: 24–5) says:

> The structure must be seen from the standpoint of the individual and
> the network of interpersonal relations surrounding him. A man divided
> the inhabitants of his locality into those who belonged to his security
> circle – those with whom he had safe relationships – and those who did
> not. His security circle included all bilateral kin up to fourth ascending
> generation together with other people with whom he had normally no
> blood ties but specific contractual relationships; trade partners; persons
> with whom he exchanged pigs; and affines to whom he gave or from

whom he received periodic instalments of bride price ... The members of a man's security circle could be scattered anywhere in his locality because of the land tenure system ... their garden plots were often in different quarters. To use them all they had regularly to move from one settlement to another. The members of a patrilineage were rarely localized and hamlets consisted of irregular clusters of people, some of whom were interrelated and others not ... A leader's authority was always ill-defined: he could not represent a specific group, but only the often transient inhabitants of his own and possibly neighbouring hamlets. Dispersal of land holdings and consequent migration enabled his followers to divide their allegiance between him and his rivals, or withdraw it immediately if his prowess was eclipsed.

The possibilities of shifting allegiances and the confusion of social categories are beautifully described. The Garia traded with other tribes having variant forms of the same general type of social organization. As Lawrence says:

Nobody in any of the societies outlined clearly understood its total structure. Rather, individuals conducted their affairs from a purely egocentric standpoint: in terms of constellations of person-to-person relationships, some denoting membership of a descent or local group, and others affinal, cognatic, exchange, or trade ties. (ibid.: 28)

He goes on to describe the universe in which these people saw themselves. It was an optimistic view. The world existed for man and he had the right to enjoy it. It could be manipulated according to straightforward rules, very comparable in their effectiveness to the rules of reciprocity by which men compelled one another to exchange goods and women. Religion was a technology for overcoming risk. There was no moral feedback in the system, he remarks with a tinge of surprise.

Spiritual values such as purity and sin were non-existent. There was no idea of rewards in the next world in return for good works or of separate destinations for 'good' and 'bad'. The affairs of the dead automatically regulated themselves. Even the initiatory taboos had no abstract ethical meaning. (loc. cit.)

It was an extremely pragmatic religion.

Spatially . . . the cosmos was conceived as a unified physical realm with virtually no supernatural attributes; in which human beings reacted not only with each other but also with deities, spirits and totems. (ibid.: 31)

The characteristics of a successful man were personal pre-eminence and secret ritual knowledge.

The leaders were men who 'really knew' and who could direct the activities of others – those who did not 'really know' – to the best advantage. It was popular conviction of this ability that enabled the particularly successful leader, who had an outstanding personality and had never been defeated by unforeseen circumstances, to lure followers away from his less fortunate rivals. (loc. cit.)

Here we have a brief glimpse of the religion we would expect to correspond to this kind of social structure. Power is located so as to be theoretically available for all, but it needs a talented man to go out and get it for himself according to known rules. The cosmos is amoral. Attitudes to ritual are highly magical. It is an ego-focused religion, as predictable in an ego-focused social structure.

I now quote from another Melanesian study. The 'Are'are, about 5,000 of them, inhabit the south of the island of Malaita. Daniel de Coppet points out that their residential rules and land rights do not admit of description in terms usually adopted by anthropologists. Over a vast mountainous area, funeral sites are fixed points of reference around which individuals circulate. For rights of cultivation are determined by genealogical links with these sites. One can choose among all and any of one's ancestors. So each person has a wider range of choice. There is no word to signify territorial boundary; there is no inside nor outside of a local territory. Only genealogically defined positions relative to funeral sites are significant. Men are not enclosed within any kinds of bounded territories. Like many other Melanesians, the 'Are'are use a form of shell or tooth money for expressing their relationships. These are worked out in a complex pattern of trade and ritual exchanges.

Each individual carries a certain number of elements which assure him power over the world and over his peers. First, his identity in the form of several names of which some come to him from his father's side and some from his mother's. From birth, he holds defined land rights, and will receive on the death of each of his parents a share in their property. He will also be able to use his technical knowledge and his knowledge of moral, ritual and social rules, and supernatural powers inherited or bought. Finally, he is responsible for all the credits and debts which he creates in the course of ceremonial exchanges. (de Coppet, 1968)

From this common starting point the 'Big Man' imposes himself as leader, without any special titles, without the framework of any hierarchy or installation, no special rights to levy taxes or to demand labour. It is a purely personal achievement. His power rests only in the consent of his followers. But the more numerous they are, the greater his prestige and power. Here is basically the same social situation. A relation of reciprocity and interdependence, a premise of initial equality and an actual pattern of gross inequality. Everyone else depends on the Big Man for their livelihood and security. He creates the political and ritual framework in which ordinary men can work out their cycles, patterns of reciprocal exchanges in grander and grander patterns. His glory enhances the lustre of theirs. He creates large-scale local alliances, controls violence, settles disputes. He does it all by generosity, hard work, skilful manipulation of the rules of feast-giving and compensation. The rules are immensely complex. For him a ladder of achievement, for those whose only hope of freedom is to give up the struggle for solvency and esteem, they are an oppressive grid.

Another good example of this kind of social system was given by Oliver for the Siuai of Bougainville Island, in the Solomons (1957). Here again, a highly individualistic, competitive society is lifted above a lowly level of achievement by the efforts of individual Big Men. The leaders compete for followers, force other men to extend themselves to their utmost capacity to produce yams, pigs and all manner of standard luxuries for feasts at which they challenge and discountenance their rivals. The successful leader challenges the leader of the next club-house; then, successful in his own district, he challenges the leader of another district. Each success rebounds to the glory of his own club-house. If he had not asserted himself, they would have apathetically half-exploited their environment. There would have been no excitement and no collaboration. During the period of his prime, they reach a higher level of organization than they would otherwise have been capable of. When he grows old there is the natural fall-off of his following. Somewhere else some other leader arises and the level of social organization rises there, while it falls here. Everyone in this society knows that it is only personal qualities which help a leader. Their cosmos expresses this precisely by attributing to each man his own set of spiritual lieutenants. The Big Man has the fiercest, biggest demons to work for him (ibid.: 444–6). Gradually we build up the picture from these cultures of a type of society very preoccupied with success. The man who works well for himself benefits everyone else. It is a system based on private enterprise, and highly cultivated managerial skills. The cosmos is morally neutral and basically optimistic. Anyone can reach out of the sky any Excalibur magic sword he is big enough to wield. There is no disapproval of men who use magic to further their own cause. Where the ends are approved, the means are also approved. The admired virtues are ambition, cunning and strength. Not all New Guinea societies conform closely to this pattern. For example, K. Burridge (1965) describes the Tangu of Northern Madang District as also seeing their universe as amoral (p. 225), magical (p. 246), unpredictable and capricious (pp. 239–40), but he describes here much greater emphasis on sorcery fears. Meggitt describes the Mae Enga of the Western Highlands (1965) as dominated by their fears of ancestral ghosts. Both societies seem to exhibit the features we would predict from the foregoing argument: smaller and more closed groups for the sorcery-ridden Tangu, and an ascribed patrilineal role-system with well-defined local communities for the ancestor-fearing Mae Enga. But only a close examination of the way grid and group are felt in tribes in a single cultural area will throw light on these variations.

I now take an example from Europe. In the typical cosmology of the ego-focused social system power is an individual gift. Supernatural power is attributed in such a way as to validate individual success and explain individual failure. Thus among our Teutonic forbears, luck was the dominant cosmological idea, as destiny was among the ancient Greeks.

Recall that the Teutons had a cognatic system of kinship in which obligations of help were reckoned to radiate out from each individual in all lines of descent. Then read Grönbech's account in *The Culture of the Teutons* (1931):

> Whichever way we turn, we find the power of luck. It determines all progress. Where it fails, life sickens. It seems to be the strongest power, the vital principle indeed of the world. (Vol. I: 127)

He goes on to describe the capricious and individual nature of this power. Each family might claim a certain kind of luck, for sailing, or fighting or fishing. King Eric Weatherhat had the wind in his hat: he could change it by turning it about.

> Among chieftains, this gift of victory shows in its full splendour. We find men of military genius, who bring victory in their train wherever they go. All the Norwegian kings of Harald Fairhair's race had this great gift of victory. And when Carl Hakon was able to fill for a time the place as a ruler over Norway, it was due not least to his luck in winning victories, in pursuing and killing. It kept the people on his side, for they held that no one could be like him in respect of this particular gift. A like tone is apparent in the opening of the story of Beowulf, about Hrothgar's kingdom; unto him was given war-speed and battle honour, so that his kinsmen followed him until the younglings were waxen and gathered about him in their host ... 'And when they saw their leader was fallen, they fled every man' – this sentence occurs again and again in the sagas, and its truth is confirmed again and again by history. If the great man's war-luck failed, what could the lesser luck of lesser men avail? (loc. cit.)

I am struck with how closely in many respects Professor Maurice Freedman's accounts of Chinese geomancy correspond to the picture I have been building up of a cosmology appropriate to a highly individualistic, competitive social system. In his presidential address to the Royal Anthropological Institute, 1968, he describes the Feng-shui system, the geomancy of buildings. A building modifies the landscape, and so disturbs a complex balance of forces. The landscape is part of a system, any change in the form of one element may be to the detriment of others, so that the geomancer's task is to divine the best relation for his client, whether that be a village community as a whole or any individual member of it. The landscape suggests certain symbols, such as dragons, writing brushes.

> The sinking of a well or the cutting of a road is likely to sever a dragon's artery or sinew (to take the commonest case) and release some terrible power of misfortune to issue in poverty, disease or childlessness. A road made to lead straight to my door is an arrow against which I shall be able to protect myself only with difficulty and perhaps at great expense ... The link between the general properties of a site and the fate of those who occupy it lies in the horoscope ... the geomancer charged with the job of finding and using sites for particular clients is engaged, on his client's behalf, in carving out their best possible future, in staking the best possible claim for them in a world of restricted opportunities. For happiness and prosperity are not limitless; they form a fixed fund from which each man must strive to draw the maximum for himself at the expense of others. (Freedman, 1969)

Here is a fascinatingly complex variant of the cosmology of competition. Whereas the New Guinea and Teutonic models deal in unlimited opportunity, the Chinese one is restricted and competition all the more keenly pursued. It is, moreover, adapted to a literate and numerate society of scholars. But, these big differences apart, it is also morally neutral, a manipulable system, ego-focused as the others. I would expect its use to vary according to the importance of ascribed status in different sectors of society. Maurice Freedman gives an old myth of a geomancer who tried to overthrow the Ming dynasty by ensuring that his own burial site would place his son in the position of becoming Emperor. But the son had to follow certain precise instructions and to wait a prescribed number of days of mourning. His impatience led him to cut the mourning time short by one day, and so all the well-laid plans, which depended on exact timing, went awry. Thus a moral and social limit on the powers of geomancy can be imported into an otherwise amoral technology. I would also expect the whole feeling of the art to change between periods of restriction to periods of expansion, or between sectors of society which sense themselves to be expanding or shut in. In the expanding social system Feng-shui should be surely an optimistic art, but the geomancer should find his clientele falling off. In the restricted system his business would thrive on the fears, well-grounded, of his clients. There would be more tendency to consult, more readiness to alter graves and buildings, less happy-go-lucky, do-it-yourself assurance about the generally propitious elements in the landscape. Our own industrial consultants find within limits that economic stringency is good for their class of business.

We have no difficulty in finding models for the competitive cosmology in the industrial world. If we look for men who see the world as a morally neutral, technical system which is lying there for themselves to exploit with their own special gifts, in which they place great confidence, we find them in any of our great industrial magnates. I select Lord Thomson of Fleet, whose biography is so engagingly frank and detailed on all the relevant points (Braddon, 1965). The wide range of his geographical movements between his childhood home in Toronto and his present London head office suggests a parallel with the possibilities of free movement within the New Guinea societies I have described. The increasing geographical scale of his responsibilities ranks him, on the same standards, as a very Big Man indeed. His obsession with making money, then his obsession with gaining a peerage – it is all very recognizably like the New Guinea ambition to enjoy power, dependants and prestige. From a clerical post in the Colonial Cordage Company, to proprietor of 140 newspapers, here is someone who has never submitted to the pressure of group boundaries, local or other. His responsibility is to himself and his own immediate family. When challenged by victims of his enterprise as to the morality of his action, closing down or amalgamating failing businesses, he would be always ready with 'Someone has to foot the wages bill'. What was good for him was also best for the majority, and for the growing number of his dependants.

First, I would like to show by quotations why he should be classed as someone free from group constraints. His career is marked by close partnerships, but, of those he started out with, very few survived to share his final triumph. Family apart, his personal relationships are largely mechanized; the majority of his contacts are fleeting and impersonal.

> From 1953 to 1957 his diaries reveal a profusion of entries that read 'Dinner jacket, speak 20 minutes' – a profusion which is matched only by the scarcity of his private or informal engagements.

At receptions, night after night,

> He would shed the hat and the black loose-swinging overcoat, and talk and grin amongst the throng. Yet seem always solitary: with – rather than of – a group. (ibid.: 265)

This is a man who sends Christmas cards every year to everyone he ever knew (p. 276) and whose secretary brings him a weekly set of birthday greetings to sign for dispatch to a long list of names. He has thrust his way up through a series of statuses, his eye unashamedly on the top grades which stood as challenges.

> I want to find out if I'm as good as I think I am ... What I want more than anything in the world is a Knighthood. (ibid.: 169)

> On the subject of his peerage he confessed: 'This title has always been an even greater ambition than owning a hundred newspapers because it seemed such an unreasonable one – a hundred million-to-one chance.' (ibid.: 311)

Clearly the more unreasonable the ambition, the more attractive it seems. With a longer life-span he might have tried for Shah of Persia. Very interested in rank, enjoying being called Roy by all his employees, but anxious to be correct in observing the social rules:

> 'Say, Roy, ... is there anyone here who's just plain mister?' 'Only you'n me,' Thomson told him happily. He was going through a period when the mere presence of aristocracy made him feel happy – and

tonight, at this private dinner party, he had landed one duke, five earls and a veritable mob of knights. (ibid.: 207)

Within these circles he protected himself by ensuring that he was well-briefed. ('Say, how do I address this guy? Is it My Lord or My Lord Bishop?'). (ibid.: 273)

The existence of a set of formal relationships and ranks provides for him a framework on which to develop his ego-centred field of activity. His social universe is to be manipulated by energy and scrupulous observance of rules.

Asked what might happen to the man who did not make a 10% profit on money he had borrowed at 5%, Thomson's reply was simple. The bank had no right to lend to anyone so half-witted. (ibid.: 185)

And, right from the start, we see 'im always poring over his balance-sheets. Like the game of snakes and ladders, the balance-sheets represent rules which send him to the winning post and his rivals to the starting point. His dynamism and attitudes to time and work are characteristic:

At his first board meeting he opened proceedings punctually at 10 a.m. and at 2.30 p.m. was still hard at it. 'Doesn't this fellow have any sense of time?' a hungry director asked Chapman irritably. 'Not when there's work to be done,' Chapman told him. Between them, Chapman and Thomson made clear that budgeting and rationalizing were to be imposed on the well-established chaos of the *Scotsman*'s finances. (ibid.: 171)

We also see the pragmatic approach to morality: it pays to be honest is a solemn principle (pp. 236, 273). He is, by admission, not a religious man. Interviewed on television:

'Are you a religious man?'
'No, I'm afraid I am not.'
'Do you have a nominal religion that you support?'
'Yes, I'm a Protestant, loosely speaking. I would go to any Protestant church.'
'You have a conventional belief in God?'
'Quite so.'
'Do you think it is possible for a man who has done as well out of the wicked world as you have to say that he lives the life of a Christian?'

'I think in all respects,' Thomson retorted uncompromisingly. 'Yes! I believe implicitly in the Golden Rule. "Do unto others as you would have them do unto you." ' (ibid.: 275–6)

It is pleasing to think of Lord Thomson in the guise of a New Guinea hero: the feasts, the balance-sheets, the dynamism, it all makes the same sense, whether newspapers are bought with money, or pigs with shells. Oliver gives these glimpses of a genial Siuai leader:

A clever man like Soηi makes plans for pig-collecting years in advance. Orim said of him: 'Other men sit in the clubhouse and chew betel nut, talking of nothing. Not so with Soηi. His heart is full of pigs and shell money; giving this and receiving that; enlarging his following, emphasizing his *potu* (renown) and dividing his *anurara*' (shell-cash). And after a great feast, to make a success of which his followers have slaved for weeks and are now lying round exhausted, he gives them no rest. Yet early next morning the wooden gongs boomed out again and they seemed louder than ever, probably because the noise was so unexpected. A few sleepy natives strolled in the direction of the club house and heard Soηi storm out: 'Hiding in your homes again, copulating night and day while there's work to be done! Why, if it were left up to you, you would spend the rest of your lives smelling yesterday's pigs. But I tell you, yesterday's feast was nothing. The next one will be really big. Sihan, I want you to arrange with Konu for his largest pig; and you, Maimoi, go to Mokakaru and find a pig for Uremu; and . . . etc.' (Oliver, 1949: 25)

So the work of organizing credit and partnerships for the next take-over feast never stops. Whenever a newspaper is bought there is a feast in Thomson's diary and plenty of smaller, preparatory feasts. One could justly account all the rest of his activities as preparations for more and more splendid feasts. The strict relevance of the New Guinea parallel is plain enough.

Among the cosmologies of success we should recognize different kinds of control exerted over the individual's behaviour. Chinese geomancy for example, itself a technique free of moral consideration, is part of a complex system in which moral controls are fully represented in the idea of Heaven. The Teuton's idea of personal success was moderated by the close relation between luck and honour. But it is possible for personal success to be celebrated without recognizing any other constraints than those written into the rules of the game. In industrial society a limited moral basis for transactions is supplied by the recognition that financial probity and creditworthiness are necessary for success. In New Guinea a leader's dependence on his followers creates a sensitive feedback system. Everyone who transacts with others subscribes to the respect for reciprocity, and feels as sensitive to shame as to glory. These moral restraints are generated in the competition itself. Though they inform the concept of the upright man, the honest broker, they do nothing further to relate the individual to any final purposes of the community as such.

Here we seem to have a type of social system without a collective conscience. Lowie did well to point to its existence, adducing the rank individualism of Crow religion as a type which Durkheim's approach could not accommodate (1925). This is the very type of society which Durkheim thought could not exist in primitive economic conditions: low level of economic interdependence combined with highly competitive individualism, and a religion of private guardian spirits for each man. In this system, whether among the American Indians or in New Guinea or here amongst ourselves, each person is committed to it by the lure of outstanding success (or even just moderate success) for himself.

If we turn to consider how a social group can weld the symbols of self and society into a coherent whole, it appears that the ego-focused grid system does nothing comparable for the concept of self. Questions about the identity and value of the self are hardly soluble except by manifestations of success. And the system of strong grid is such that only the few can achieve success. For these few it is possible to find that the rules are so many ropes and ladders for a giddy emancipation. For the majority of others it may never be clear that the path is blocked for themselves: one day their luck or demons may become more effective. But there must always be some who discover that they are born to lose all their lives, to serve for a pittance, to admire glittering prizes which can never come within their grasp. Who are the bad sorcerers so much disapproved by respectable New Guinea society, the stranglers with red eyes and long nails whose hearts are said to be consumed with jealousy? The good men use sorcery all the time as part of the approved technology of success. So the disapproved sorcerers must be the failures, the drop-outs, casualties of the system. What their world view is, what they think of the way the rules are worked, how they view the system would be the most valuable information of all for our comparison. How do *they* succeed in protecting their image of their inner selves from degradation and disgust? It is possible that they come to believe in their own moral inadequacy and take their own bitterness and jealousy as proof of the soundness of accusations levelled against them. Or are these the men waiting to be delivered by a new cargo cult? The ethnography of the world seen from the eyes of the accused sorcerer has not been recorded as yet.

Curiously enough, the successful leaders, having spiralled free of personal constraints, emerge into a rarified atmosphere which has something in common with the world view of the people most heavily subject to controlling pressure in the same society. Their ephemeral social contacts and imperviousness to personal pressures enable them to see the cosmos as a rational order not dominated by people but by manipulable objects. These objects are the impersonal rules which govern their transactions. Their world is not controlled by independent ghosts and witches, or evil men. There is no sin: only stupidity. Human nature is divided between the foolish and the wise, between 'those who know', and the others. They feel no need for symbolic action other than triumphal feasts for symbolizing the control of society by the self. Hence, a certain blindness to any symbolic representations of the self being controlled by society which mysteriously transcends it and vests it with greater significance. For them it is a rational world whose laws are perfectly intelligible and unmysterious. And it is, on the whole, a satisfactory world, for those successful leaders.

In New Guinea, this social structure, an ego-focused grid, and this cosmology, are the permanent, on-going back-drop to recurring cargo cults. The term 'cargo' represents European wealth, clothes, food and trade goods. The essence of these cults is that some mythical hero will reveal to the people secret rituals for obtaining cargo. Periodically, at the say-so of a prophet, they drop their hoes, destroy their property, perform rituals and go out to the wharf or airfield to await the delivery of the cargo. Cargo cults have caused great turmoil and administrative concern in Melanesia; mobs are controlled with violence, leaders jailed. Yet they are only driven underground and recur again and again. There is now a considerable literature on these cults. Inevitably, since cargo is a word and an idea derived from European occupation the cults have been analysed as colonial manifestations, the result of contact with a foreign culture (Lawrence, 1964; Worsley, 1957; Thrupp, 1962: 17). But it seems very possible that similar movements have occurred earlier, though at less regular intervals.

The modern cargo cult is very like other millennial movements. It discards existing rituals and looks for a radical new rite which will usher in a golden era. But it has one distinctive and crucial mark. Most millennial movements reject the material values of society and seek to transform it into something quite other. But the cargo cult explicitly accepts the current material values, these especially, and seeks to provide for its followers a means of achieving them. The difference corresponds to two distinctive attitudes to poverty in contemporary Christian religion. On the one hand is the Sermon on the Mount, blessing poverty and warning against riches, on the other is the vow to abolish poverty and achieve affluence for all. Its drastic contemporary form may well be an adaptation to a particularly prolonged and acute contemporary crisis of an ancient ritual of moral regeneration. The present crisis is caused by the coastal Melanesians finding themselves in relation with rich foreigners with whom they cannot transact because they have nothing to offer in exchange. They are therefore unable to enter into reciprocal relations with the Europeans. They find themselves denied the basic human rights of social intercourse, and denied it by people with whom they would particularly like to transact. This sense of being excluded, disregarded, of being made to feel of no value is a regular experience in the system of strong grid. For continually as one man rises to eminence he reduces his former partners to insignificance, refuses to trade with them or to feast with them as equals, and sets his sights on other more lucrative relationships. Lawrence very convincingly describes the cargo cult as an attempt to adopt traditional ritual techniques to the European situation. In this everyday magic a Garia man sought to make other people 'think on' him. To get someone to 'think on' oneself is to get them to co-operate. Social oblivion is the great risk. This idiom of forcing other people by ritual to 'think on' one is a telling way of expressing the anxiety not to be neglected and disparaged in a system where only some can succeed and where the rest are bound to experience disparagement and, with it, material and social loss.

The content of these social relationships can be described as the exchange of equivalent goods and services. A purely nominal relation had little value. What counted was that each party to a relationship should be forced to 'think on' . . . the other by the fulfilment of specific obligations – as in kinship and exchange commitments – which demanded an automatic and equal return at the risk of losing personal reputation and mutual advantage . . . where there was no exchange of goods and services, there could be no sense of relationship, mutual obligation and value, but only suspicion, hostility and risk of warfare. (Lawrence, 1964: 29–30)

Cargo, then, is not wanted for its own sake, but for the new relationships it will permit, when Papuan can exchange with European on fair and equal terms. The cargo cult is to be seen as a specially potent rite which dissolves all existing commitments and relationships for the sake of establishing a new, more profitable set of links. Not surprisingly, in view of what we have seen about the tendency to reproduce a social situation in bodily symbolism, shaking, frenzy and sexual promiscuity accompany many cargo cult rituals. The people want to wipe out the old system, with its inferior forms of wealth, and to make a new beginning. I find it hard to believe that very similar movements of moral regeneration have not been endemic in Melanesia long before the invention of the idea of cargo. The means by which the cults spread from one locality to the next by way of regularly instituted payments suggest a well-known system. Kenelm Burridge suggests that the Tangu had resorted to cults of renewal before the advent of Europeans (1960: 25). My own hypothesis is that a society so strongly centred on a structure of ego-focused grid is liable to recurrent breakdown from its inherent moral weakness. It cannot continually sustain the commitment of all its members to an egalitarian principle that favours a minority. It has no way of symbolizing or activating the collective conscience. One would anticipate an ego-focused grid system to swing between the glorification of successful leaders and the celebration of the right of the masses to enjoy success. Thus the cargo cult and its prototypes would be cults of revolt against the way the social structure seems to be working, but not of revolution against the traditional structure itself.

Many are struck with the parallel between student revolt and violent millennialism. Compensation theory gives as the cause insecurity or deprivation. But my own hypothesis points to a lack of adequate structuring in the university population. It could well be that academics, in a given department, could feel hemmed in together in competitive disorder and show themselves prone to diagnose in terms of the witch hunt. And it could well be that the students themselves experience grid without group. Each, with an individual time-table controlling every hour of his day, moves from impersonal lecture halls to isolated lodging; the groups he joins are fragmentary and short-term. The organization to which he is subject seems to prevent him from realizing his aspirations instead of securing them for him. He experiences society as an alien, sinister body, a machine which represses life. His categories of pollution and purity, of matter and mind, flesh and spirit are drawn up on the age-old pattern. Hence the brutal confrontation: his teachers live in one universe, they cherish boundaries and smell conspiracy against sacred forms; he lives in another universe in which no particular form is sacred; form as such is distinct from content and inferior to it; he opposes classification as the expression of empty form, the very emblem of evil. While I am writing this the University of Illinois is investigating the destruction of its library catalogues and deploring an apparently mindless attack on learning. But the destruction of categories of any kind is a symbolic act which replicates social life over-structured by grid, the experience which has always driven people to value unstructured personal experiences and to place their faith in a catastrophic event which will sweep away all existing forms of structure.

To sum up: the four social types we have identified by grid and group have four distinctive cosmological types. First, for high classification, where grid and group are strong, the universe is just. Pain and suffering are either the proper punishments of individual misdeeds or accounted by transcendental book-keeping so that the effects of one man's virtue are chalked up for the common good and his faults are likewise charged to the community. It is a complex regulative cosmos.

Second, for the social type I have called small group, the universe is divided between warring forces of good and evil. Leadership is precarious in such groups, roles ambiguous and undefined. The group boundary is the main definer of rights: people are classed either as members or strangers. Magical danger is associated with the idea of boundary. Evil is a foreign danger introduced by foreign agents in disguise. Group members accuse deviants in their midst of allowing the outside evil to infiltrate. The accusations lead to fission of the group. The cosmos is endangered by the vile, irrational behaviour of human agents of evil. It is preoccupied with rituals of cleansing, expulsion of spies or witches and the re-drawing of boundaries. Many people believe in witchcraft without being preoccupied by fear of their neighbour's aggression. I would not include their witch-beliefs, which tend to be marginal elements of their cosmology, in this category. Witch-dominated cosmologies vary in a range which corresponds to the structuring of internal roles and the openness and permeability of the external boundary.

There are clear interpretations in what I have said on witchcraft for the history of religious movements. There could be practical implications too. If a new witch-hunting terror were to appear, such as that led by Joe McCarthy in America in the 1950s, it would not be enough to denounce him and his followers. Richard

Rovere says: 'McCarthy drew into his following most of the zanies and zombies and compulsive haters who had followed earlier and lesser demagogues.' But when witch fantasies occur on a national scale, they are not merely the product of the crazed and weak-minded and of cynical manipulators, as Arthur Miller's *The Crucible* implied. Witch hunting develops in a specifiable social niche: important factions, externally distinct, internally competitive. It could be important to adjust the conditions in which political power is sought and wielded if witch-hunting movements are to be controlled.

It is unlikely that a diplomat who nears the top of his profession is spiralling freely in the buccaneering environment of the Big Men. Nor can one assume that the conditions of the Foreign Service reproduce necessarily the ordered and predictable system of strong grid and group where precedence is bolstered by piety. It could be that the confusion and uncertainty of the small Central African village or of a sect such as the Plymouth Brethren in their early days afford a closer model. If this were so, the conspiracy theory of politics would fog the atmosphere of summit meetings with suspicion and experts would urge their leaders to outcast evil-doers and draw tight on the boundaries of the good society.

Now for the third social type, the competitive leaders who dominate the system of strong grid. I have just described their success cosmology, with its syncretism and scope for private magic. For lack of recognizing this as a distinctive type, the early anthropologists may have completely misinterpreted their findings. The Dobu Islanders have long provided the stereotype of a witch-dominated cosmology. Among these far-ranging traders much respected and even feared by distant partners, each man has his own collection of formulae for success and competes passionately against his neighbours and kinsmen. It would be worth re-analysing Fortune's great pioneering study with a view to deciding whether the Dobuans are to stay classed as nervous inward-turning paranoiacs obsessed by fear of persecution or as bold tycoons who protect their magical recipes as so many industrial secrets for use against their rivals.

Fourth, the other end of the strong grid where the mass of the people are subject to impersonal rules – this type would be likely to go through successive phases according to the ups and downs of the Big Men's fortunes and according to whether their allegiance is strongly sought or disregarded. At one phase in his career, a rising leader will be attracting dependants, promising them rewards, flattering followers with his concern. This phase for the society constituted around him is like a rising trend in the level of employment. Unfilled vacancies create optimism and the followers will not find the rules of the system meaningless for their own lives since its rewards come within their reach. When riding at the top of his career the leader may have taken up most of the potential market of followers. The system is suspended thus as long as his drive and ability holds it together. There could be a phase something like over-employment in which the followers gain such a sense of worth that they dare to play the market, look round for a better leader, switch allegiance. Even so, there will always be some who find themselves in all phases holding the wrong end of the stick. No one says that this is a comfortable or dignified system in which to grow old. At some stage inevitably the leader himself ages and loses his grip. The machinery clogs. The best of the followers are seduced away by stronger leaders. In the middle of the rival empires, a mass of people are uncertain of their future. Others are too deeply embedded in one man's fortunes and have done too well by him to be acceptable in another camp. The confusion and crisis would be like the experience of Europe as the Renaissance princedoms collapsed (Trevor-Roper). And in this condition, as in Europe, the idea of the millennium, ever present in the consciousness from infancy, begins to come forward. The very structure of strong grid predisposes the rank and file to millennial movements. This society, spanning the whole diagram from right to left, creates at the left side the extremely pragmatic, unspeculative and materialist belief system and on the right a tendency, alternately repressed and breaking out, to millennialism.

Having set out these four social systems and their distinctive beliefs, I have to pay attention to a factor which has already confused the simplicity of the design, the factor I have called sparsity. Ultimately the trends on the right side of the diagram are aspects of human control, either by classification, or by direct personal pressures, or both, and they are accentuated by tightening of the control. It follows then that if there are very few people on the ground and they meet each other infrequently and irregularly and their possibilities of evading one another's company are good, there is a lessening of control. So sparsity all round is likely to have the same effect as a shift towards zero. To the right the cosmos is more punishing, to the left more benign. Decreasing human contact tends to give the same result. Hence any form of dropping out which is a dropping away from other peoples' categories and pressures gives a rosier tinge to the world. The deeper the retreat, the greater the faith in the inner purity and goodness of the human heart; the need for ritual forms is weakened, also the sense of sin.

9   Control of Symbols

According to the Book of Genesis our ancestor fell from a state of natural innocence when he ate the ambiguous fruit. To attain knowledge of good and evil is still the god-defying and distinctive goal of human beings. And always we find ourselves unable to bear the knowledge, and always erecting filters to protect the idea of our own interior innocence. One such filter is the strong resistance made by many scholars to the very notion of social determinants of belief. They would rather think of beliefs floating free in an autonomous vacuum, developing according to their own internal logic, bumping into other ideas by the chance of historical contact and being modified by new insights. This is an inverted materialism. In the name of the primacy of mind over matter, its adherents evade their own responsibility for choosing the circumstances for their intellectual freedom. To ensure autonomy of mind we should first recognize the restrictions imposed by material existence. This leads back to our original programme.

We have identified distinctive social patterns and the theory of justification that goes with each and sustains it. Two tasks remain. One is to distinguish what is said from what is not said in each world view. Each theory has its hidden implications. These are its unspoken assumptions about the nature of ultimate reality. They are unspoken because they are taken for granted. There is no need to make them explicit because this is the common basis of experience. Such shared assumptions underlie any discourse, even the elaborated speech code which is developed to inspect them. They are the foundations on which social reality is constituted, as the phenomenologists point out. Yet so far, though it is agreed that reality is a social construct (Berger and Luckmann), no convincing order has been discerned in all the multiple kinds of reality construable. To find what is implicit in each cosmology we shall follow the same thread that has un-ravelled the rest of the argument, the relation of self to society. By this thread we shall find how the grand building blocks of the cosmos are balanced together and so fathom the gaps be-tween them. The unspoken assumptions betray how the social bond is constituted in the secret consciousness of individuals. With that exposed, the scene is set for the last task, the relation between the media and the society whose visible substance they are.

Each social form and its accompanying style of thought restricts the self-knowledge of the individual in one way or another. With strong grid and group, there is the tendency to take the intellectual categories which the fixed social categories require as if they were God-given eternal truths. The mind is tied hand and foot, so to speak, bound by the socially generated categories of culture. No other alternative view of reality seems possible. A small shift in the definitions is anathema and worth protecting with bloodshed. Anomaly is abhorrent. In such a system, the purity code has set up a strong distinction between the private and the public, and its wider implications are irresis-tible. Here the eruption of the organic into the social domain is most dangerous, to be purified with ritual. The individual in transition from one social status to another is like matter out of place, impure and to be ritually re-integrated. Rituals have the function of celebrating the transcendance of the whole over the part.

By contrast, still in the right-hand quadrant, any position near zero is less impressed by the purity rule and its meanings. But charming though its world view is, and rosy its concept of human nature, it is a temporary resting place which turns barren for the long-term resident. All opportunities of individual develop-ment are limited by the lack of organization. The range and quality of personal interaction are restricted. The possibilities of knowing the self are reduced by the limited contact with other selves. Intellectually it is as null as it is ineffective in organization.

Second, the closed community with its intolerance of imperfections: its focus on an impossible good is limiting in another way. The failure to confront the menacing idea of evil is as complete here as in the first case. At zero point evil is implicitly ignored, here it is explicitly shunned and rejected. Thus both systems allow the individual to cherish an inadequate view of the self and its capacities and dangers.

Third, the strong grid: this society allows all the possibilities of large-scale organization to be taken, but at the expense of personal relationships. Again, in the extreme form, there is a sterile exaltation of the self in isolation from other selves. Other persons are treated as things, instruments, pawns in a game. So the individual caught up in this system is incapable of reflecting on the nature of the self, or of symbolizing it as a complex agent. Here we have an equal impoverishment of the symbolic life and deadening of metaphysical curiosity.

If we turn to the quadrant of social structures we can now draw out some general characters, some elementary types of cosmology. Take first the effects of group boundedness. To the left

Diagram 6: From Impersonal to Personal

of zero, on the horizontal axis of control, the cosmos is seen as if dominated by impersonal powers and principles. Anthropomorphism in these religions is weak. In so far as demons or gods are considered to be at all influential, they are only faintly drawn in the human image. They tend to be bizarre, dislocated or diffuse in their presence. Recall the idea of the forest as a cosmic force in the religion of Ituri pygmies, the various confused refractions through which the Nuer God is manifested, the animal spirits of the Plains Indians, to realize the extent to which anthropomorphism can be diminished. At the same time these religions are not moral regulators. They hold out no system of rewards and punishment, neither in this world nor in the next. At top left, the principles which govern the universe act as multipliers of human success or failure. It is a system of positive feedback which offers total escalation to those who are strong enough to play by the rules. And total degradation to those who fail. No techniques of re-integration and reconciliation are provided, since there is no conception of offence against the community, only of failure. There are no over-arching doctrines of sin and atonement. In these societies, the idea of the self is free from social constraint. The self is valued uniquely for its own sake, not for any contribution it can make to the whole.

On the other side of the vertical line, where group is strong, we find the opposite holds good. The powers that control the universe are modelled on human figures. Either they are the spirits of dead fathers and grandfathers, or culture heroes like big brothers, or a creator god, the most ancestral figure of them all. Or they are actual, real human beings, free men with powers to bless and curse, or witches and sorcerers with their own armoury of ill-doing. On this side, where group is strong, social control is built into the cosmos. These humans and human-like powers are activated by moral situations. Ancestors punish and reward; curses avenge moral wrong; even witches only strike when provoked by neglect or rudeness. The idea of the self is surrounded with prickly moral contexts in which it has to operate.

Now to consider the vertical axis. Here we have a very different set of discriminations. Diminishing grid gives a pattern for increasingly ascetic behaviour. Where grid is strong the external manifestations of life are positively valued. Wealth and pomp are justified as symbolic expressions or as good in themselves. There is no feeling of guilt about spending; the outward expressions of

Diagram 7: From Asceticism to Affirmation

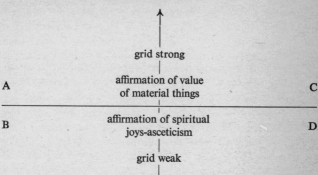

society and self are not despised or feared – the world, society, the Church, organization as such and all its signs are affirmed. As we approach zero, there are two kinds of asceticism. With strong group, ascetic attitudes express the rejection of what is external, the husk, the empty shell, the contamination of the senses. Strict controls are set on bodily enjoyment and on the gateways of sensual experience. Moving towards the zero of the horizontal line, another form of asceticism results from valuing human fellowship above material things. Those who belong in this sector are usually aware of other ways of living, both more arduous and more richly rewarded in material wealth. Their culture is often seen as a choice, a preference for the simple life. Thus the Mbuti pygmies, after a period of lush living in the Bantu village, scamper back gleefully to the forest in the spirit of children repairing to their holiday camping to enjoy candle-light and sausages. Thus the reaction against the American middle class consciously prides itself on embracing poverty.

In their personal life-style, their aesthetic sense, many in the Movement reject affluence and its associated symbols. The ambition to escape from poverty is no spur to action in their lives, . . . their parents' desire to own, to accumulate, to achieve the status and prestige which

177

go with material wealth, are meaningless goals to them . . . (Jacobs and Landau, 1966 : 15–16)

Then again, escaping more completely from social life and coming even nearer to zero, we hear Thoreau preaching the beauty of nature from his hermitage at Walden. If the active society listens to the hermit, our diagram's rules will shift him out from zero to the bottom left with the other voices in the wilderness which cry out and are heeded. Then the range between society and renunciation becomes more than a passive scale of measurement. A dialogue involves two sectors of society, the renouncers reproaching the celebrators with the vanity of their ways. The whole diagram becomes too complicated when the precepts of the renouncers are accepted by society at large and come to control the idiom of public classification. Just such a competitive dialogue is analysed between the Brahmans and the renouncing sects of India by Louis Dumont who traces to it the root ideas of Hinduism. A parallel dialogue between Rome and the succession of desert dwellers, anchorites and poor friars has complicated our own culture. We cannot but be aware of the ascetic tradition.

Already the comparison of world views has led to life-styles. I have started the second task which is to relate the media of expression to cosmology and social structure. Without more ado, we are ready to answer our questions about the social conditions in which ritual comes into contempt. We took ritual to signify fixed forms of communication which acquire magical efficacy. The top half of our diagram represents the main body of society. The further away from zero in all directions upwards, the stronger the belief in efficacious signs; the closer to zero the less the demand for communication, and the less the tendency to vest symbols with something more than an expressive function. Magicality is a product of social control. To insist that the symbols are efficacious is to threaten blasphemy and sacrilege with automatic danger and to promise the reverent automatic blessing. Magicality is an instrument of mutual coercion which only works when common consent upholds the system. Useless for a witch doctor to invest a fetish with magic power by the sole authority of his

fringe followers and to the central figures of the cult. For the initiated Manicheean teachers themselves seem to have developed from the same doctrines a typical sectarian cosmology. Their small, tightly organized group maintained its identity by elaborate rituals, ruthless rejection of the bad outside and affirmation by symbolic means of the purity of the group and of their inner selves. To most of their educated followers they offered an intellectual freedom which they themselves did not enjoy, since they were bound by the authority of Mani. But their system of moral control and bodily asceticism offered a technique for achieving mastery over the self.

Finally, there is another source of anti-ritualism. The subject followers of distant leaders in the strong grid system find themselves weakly related to other people. Their social categories are barely defined, their contracts with other people fragile and unreliable. They are in a universe dominated by principles. It is as if things, not people, determine their lot. And, as with principles and things, there is no arguing with these people in charge, no appeal to compassion. This is the subjection which is hardest to bear. The impersonal controls of weather and tides, however cruel, do not produce the sense of injustice which is aroused when people behave as if they and those they control are objects, not persons. A violent source of anti-ritualism is opened up when persons are perceived to be behind the principles, or benefiting from them.

The unsuccessful may find themselves forced to move from leader to leader in the attempt to get a better deal and as they move they break their social ties. Or they find themselves unable to move, located with other people who also would like to move but cannot, and with whom they form an undifferentiated mass. The delicate differentiations by which they structure their relations with each other are of no significance to the people who operate the rules against them. Although they themselves discriminate the claims of age, sex, relationship, these distinctions make no difference to the impersonal principles which ruthlessly separate them or force them to huddle together. What they experience is a failure of other people to recognize their claims as persons.

Persons in control behave to them mechanically and treat them as if they were objects. This, I suggest, is the experience which has always predisposed to the millennial cult, which wipes out existing rituals.

Anti-ritualism is therefore the idiom of revolt. It must be so, and it must inevitably press the case by decrying not only meaningless rituals, but all rituals as such. Even when the case demands more articulate communication, even when more meaningful rituals are needed, anti-ritualism is undiscriminating in its sweeping condemnation of formality. Here we come to Durkheim's insight that the shared experience of society structures the internal consciousness of the private person to match that of the collectivity. The public symbolic system which has been set up by social intercourse puts its controlling stamp on individual perception and restricts understanding to the possibilities admitted in its own construction of the universe. In the small group a man is caught searching under his bed for witches when he might learn more by searching his own heart. With strong grid and group, the sources of innovation are squeezed out and despised for their incompatibility with the given categories. And yet such a society may desperately be seeking new solutions to its problems. If compensation theory were valid, the masses who experience control by objects would in reaction seek to differentiate more effectively. But instead they rush to adopt symbols of nondifferentiation and so accentuate the condition from which they suffer. This is the dangerous backlash in symbolic experience of which we should beware. The man who has been raised up seeks symbols of his high estate; the one who has been degraded seeks symbols of debasement. After T. E. Lawrence had suffered humiliation he could only bear a social life to match his sense of degradation. He sought to make true in the sight of other people what he felt in himself.

From henceforward my way will lie with these fellows [in the RAF here degrading myself (for in their eyes and your eyes and Winterton's eyes I see that it is a degradation) in the hope that some day I will really feel degraded, be degraded, to their level. I long for people to look down on me and despise me, and I'm too shy to take the filthy steps which would publicly shame me, and put me into their contempt. (Knightley and Simpson, 1969: 255)

Thus we should expect that those who have the sense of living without meaningful categories, and who suffer from being treated as an undifferentiated, insignificant mass, will seek to express themselves by inarticulate, undifferentiated symbols.

They should react strongly against non-differentiation and seek to establish clear categories and distinctions which the oppressors would be forced to recognize. They should get organized. This would involve them in hierarchical discriminations. But expressive action is easier, more satisfying and may possibly have some instrumental value. So they use marches and mass protests as expressions of revolt. These may indeed be the most effective instrument for calling attention to affliction. But insidiously the symbolic mode seduces the intellect to its own estate. The drive to achieve consonance between social and physical and emotional experience envelops the mind also in its sweep. Hence the failure of revolutionary millennialists to write a programme that in any way matches the strength of their case. Hence the apparent flippancy or unserious abandon with which they pronounce their diagnosis and their remedies. It is as if the symbolic mode has overwhelmed the freedom of the mind to grapple with reality.

The cosmology which goes with the experience of mass, of undifferentiated human solidarity has a fatal attraction for those who most vehemently wish to remedy its failures. They find themselves behaving like revivalists in the effervescent stage of a new religion. They reject social differentiation and propose programmes to enhance the sense of individual worth, human warmth and spontaneity. They pay tribute to these values, announce their ultimate triumph. But so far from doing something to realize them, in past history they have led their followers into symbolic marches and crusades, usually with dire results.

In this short space I cannot elaborately document the argument. I can sum it up and illustrate it. Where grid is oppressively exerted from afar a further weakening of the delicate relationships can turn the passive cosmology into revolutionary millennialism. Norman Cohn has listed the precipitating causes of millennialism in medieval Europe (1957). Disparate though they seem (Cohn, 1962), ranging from sexual frustration to cosmic anxiety, they all stem from an aggravation of the weakness of the social structure.

But in the most populous and economically advanced areas of Europe there existed numbers of poor folk who had no such organization behind them: in the countryside landless peasants and farm hands, in the towns journeymen (who were forbidden to organize), unskilled workers (who had no guilds) and a floating population of beggars and unemployed. It was such people as these that provided the revolutionary prophets with their following. (Cohn, 1962: 39)

Catastrophe or the fear of catastrophe: e.g. the famines and plagues which preceded several popular crusades and similar movements; the massacres which preceded the mass movements of dispersed Jews towards Jerusalem. (ibid.: 40)

The areas which saw the rise of popular crusades were always those areas north of the Alps that had a relatively dense population including landless peasants; Flanders, northern France, and the Rhine valley . . . It is significant that at the time of the First Crusade of 1095 the areas which were swept by mass enthusiasm had for ten years been afflicted by famine and drought and for five years by plague, while the crusades of 1146, 1309 and 1320 were all preluded by famines. (ibid.: 34)

That millennial fervour emerges with weakness of classification is amply demonstrated in the same volume from Brazilian and Indonesian movements (Thrupp, 1962: 55–69; 80–121 and especially 80, 88, 92–3).

For our own contemporary experiences of this kind, it is not difficult to find comparable expressions of millennial fervour. The focus is on poverty, class and race discrimination, colonialism, and student unrest. The spokesmen in each case pin-point the same symptoms: control by humans as if by things, non-differentiation, rootlessness.

The writer of one of the most thoughtful books on the Paris riots of May and June 1968, under the pseudonym of Epistemon, asks why university students in the mid twentieth century should have taken over the role of revolutionary spearhead from the working class. For answer he gives a cogent account of the revolutionary ideas on which the universities have been fed, giving particular praise and prominence to the philosophical work of Sartre. He traces very skilfully the break-up of form in drama, in literature and philosophy down to the final undermining of confidence in knowledge, as such. Although he gives a typically Gallic priority to the evolution of ideas, and only second place to the evolution of the social structures in which they are developed, he ably discusses the rootless, marginal character of the university students' social world. This would perfectly fit my analysis if only the priority were reversed. I have already hinted how Sartre's own biography fits the diagnosis. The whole history of ideas should be reviewed in the light of the power of social structures to generate symbols of their own. These symbols deceivingly commend themselves as spiritual truths unconnected with fleshly processes of conception, thus obeying the purity rule.

The poor of America in the sixties are 'victims of a bureaucratically enforced rootlessness' due to evictions from slums; the social workers are bureaucratized, hostile, dehumanized (Harrington, 1962: 157, 120). Subject colonial peoples are discerned 'only as an indistinct mass' (Fanon, 1965: 34) and they know that this is what they are:

Henceforward, the interests of one will be the interests of all, for in concrete fact *everyone* will be discovered by the troops, *everyone* will be massacred – or *everyone* will be saved. (ibid.: 37)

The men whom the growing population of the country districts and colonial expropriation have brought to desert their family holdings circle tirelessly round the different towns hoping that one day or another they will be allowed inside. It is within this mass of humanity, this people of the shanty towns, at the core of the *lumpen-proletariat* that the rebellion will find its urban spearhead. (ibid.: 103)

The leaders of the movement for Negro emancipation find their enemies inhuman:

. . . the driver of the pick-up truck pulled up alongside. He had a face from central casting, like all the faces I had watched in newsreels spitting on little girls in Little Rock and unleashing snarling police dogs in Birmingham. (Newfield, 1966: 92)

The New Radicals

are saying that the whole society – from the academy to the anti-poverty programme – has become too bureaucratized and must be decentralized and humanized. (ibid.: 204)

Students, too, protest against bureaucracy, against exaggerated compartmentalism of study, discontinuous and truncated understanding and loss of personal attachment to the worth of study as a humanistic enterprise (ibid.: 163).

This is the evidence I take that the wide-spread revolt of the left is indeed a revolt, as it says it is, against control by humans as if by objects. So much for the underlying social experience. It receives expression in the common ritual style. It relies on the symbolic expression of the state they deplore, as a means of remedy. Their intellectual stance is a rejection of categories of all kinds, including both symbolic and functional discriminations. Harrington writes scathingly of 'the definition-makers' (ibid.: 137). The students, feeling themselves subject to an undiscriminating, mindless bureaucratic machine, reject differentiation as such.

The tragedy of millennial movements, as Norman Cohn has pointed out, is that they do not usually lead to a better society. No one would wish reform to produce an explosion which creates more misery and oppression than that which provoked the movement. Such unfruitful outcomes result from the backlash of the symbolic system. Anyone who tries to correct the unfeeling-ness of the bureaucratic machine with a revolution of feeling gives up control of the situation to natural symbols. After attacking definition as such, differentiation as such, ritual as such, it is very difficult to turn about and seek the new definitions, differentiations and rituals which will remedy the case. In the period of the Crusades, beggars and orphaned children set out to take the Holy Land from the Turks by the very power of their meekness and poverty. Contemporary observers thought that they might succeed and that a golden age would begin. But the crusaders fell into the sea and were drowned or were captured by Barbary pirates. Today, our clergy, our poor and our youth unite to take the great places by demonstrating their helplessness in non-violent parades.

This is the last source of contemporary anti-ritualism. It is clear that its protest against symbols is only against rituals of differentiation. Its social experience is as much restricted by its own symbolic forms as those other three I have already indicated. It follows that the solution to grave problems of social organization can rarely come from those who experience them. For they inevitably can only think according to the cosmological type in which their social life is cast. Therefore it behoves others to identify and resist the allurements of zero.

The millennialist is optimistic about human nature (once freed from the external machine) and about the outcome of his policies. He fuses disparate problems together and resists attempts to define and distinguish. For his single problem, overthrow of the evil system, he advocates a simple solution, usually symbolic and expected to have magical effect. He has low respect for technical processes or special knowledge. Like the fundamentalist sects, he has contempt for learning and for academic (or clerical) specialization. His organization can only work in spasmodic bursts because he rejects specialized roles as such. The time span of his thinking is erratic; the millennium will come soon and suddenly; differentiation in time is as difficult for him to envisage as other kinds of differentiation.

Millennialism is to be taken very seriously, in all its forms. The solution to the problems which provoke it is not to join the stampede. To throw overboard differentiating doctrines and differentiating rituals is to reach for the poison that symbolizes the ill. Anti-ritualists around us who feel this excitement in the air, rather than yield, should feel more practical compassion for the rootlessness and helplessness that inspire it. Then, instead of sweeping away little rituals, such as Friday abstinence, which shore up a sense of belonging and of roots, and instead of belittling the magic of priesthood and sacraments, they would turn their attention to repairing the defences of grid and group.

How to humanize the machine is the problem, not how to symbolize its dehumanizing effects. When bureaucrats hear the catchword 'equality' (a symbol of non-differentiation) they should beware, for equality, like symmetry, is a mechanical principle in its operation. It chops the human diversity of need into its own pre-ordained regularities. The way to humanize the system is to cherish particular categories. The institution which runs by strict adherence to general rules gives up its own autonomy. If it tries to adopt equality or seniority or alphabetical order or any other hard and fast principle for promotion and admission, it is bound to override the hard case. Furthermore, it is bound to abandon its traditions and so its identity and its original, special purposes. For these humanizing influences depend upon a continuity with the past, benevolent forms of nepotism, irregular charity, extraordinary promotions, freedom to pioneer in the tradition of the founders, whoever they were. Instead of anti-ritualism it would be more practical to experiment with more flexible institutional forms and to seek to develop their ritual expression.

But this would mean going into the world, mixing with corruption and sin, dirtying oneself with externals, having some truck with the despised forms, instead of worshipping the sacred mysteries of pure zero. The theologians who should be providing for us more precise and original categories of thought are busy demolishing meaningless rituals and employing the theological tool chest to meet the demands of anti-ritualists. Yet the diagram of grid and group suggests that to go where the tide sweeps them can hardly be their proper calling.

10   Out of the Cave

Plato's image of the cave on whose wall are cast the shadows we mistake for real is a popular one today. There is a heady promise in various intellectual fields of escape from the conditions of knowledge. With this promise an impossible kind of freedom is being proposed, freedom from necessity of any kind. It is preached particularly in artistic and literary circles. These are the people who have shouldered the clergy's old responsibility to care for the symbols of society. They should know that the cave is the body social mediated by the image of the other body. To emerge free from its constraints would be as feasible for the artist as for a linguistic philosopher to give up the constraints of language. Indeed the illusion of escape may well be a new kind of confinement. Bernstein's work shows us something of how our different cosmologies imprison us. The free exercise of our faculties is limited by the media of expression. There are areas of experience which can be investigated in one speech code but not another. There are social relations possible for one but not another. The range of speech codes available is part of the social environment for an individual at any given time. Since the speech code is a quality inhering in the social structure, a strong one-way casual relation seems to be implied. If pressed on the matter, presumably Bernstein would be gloomy about the prospects of ever mastering the codes and being free of their restraints. On his view we can only hope for fortunate shifts in the social structure to introduce change:

The thesis to be developed here places the emphasis on changes in the social structure as major factors in shaping or changing a given culture through their effect on the consequences of speaking . . . which speech codes are generated is a function of the system of social relations. The particular form of a social relation acts selectively on what is said, when it is said, and how it is said . . . The experience of the speakers may then be transformed by what is made significant or relevant by the different speech systems. This is a sociological argument, because the speech system is taken as a consequence of the social relation, or to put it more generally, is a quality of the social structure. (Bernstein, 1965: 151)

If we apply this beyond the case of speech to culture in general, we do not necessarily subscribe to a theory of society as infrastructure, the basic phenomenon, with culture as superstructure, mere epiphenomenon. Bernstein regards both speech and relationships as qualities of the social structure. In the latter there are at least small options for dealing with other persons in one way or another, and from selections among these small-scale social choices there can be changes in the speech codes. Bernstein would not, as I understand his thesis, deny personal creativity and cultural innovation, but would have to locate them primarily in the sphere of direct human interaction. If the same analysis were applied to all the media of communication and allowance made for their effects on the experience of the society using them, the anxiety about sociological determinism would surely be allayed. For on this view, society or culture are both abstractions, categories applied to the process which, in the last resort, consists of individuals dealing with other individuals. Furthermore the elaborated code provides a means of assessing the value of one kind of social process, the codes derived from it, and the values and principles that go with both. In the long run, the argument of this book is that the elaborated code challenges its users to turn round on themselves and inspect their values, to reject some of them, and to resolve to cherish positional forms of control and communication wherever these are available. This would seem to be the only way to use our knowledge to free ourselves from the power of our own cosmology. No one would deliberately choose the elaborated code and the personal control system who is aware of the seeds of alienation it contains. After listing some of the advantages of the restricted code, which unites speakers to kin and community, Bernstein notes:

A change of code involves changes in the *means* whereby social identity and reality are created. This argument means that educational institutions in a fluid society carry within themselves alienating tendencies. (1965: 168)

By contrast the restricted code allows a person to perceive his identity as part of his immediate social world; personal and social integration are achieved together. Here we should expect to find symbols of the human body actively expressing the solidarity of the social body. The first thing that is striking about the English working-class home is the attempt to provide privacy in spite of the difficulties of layout. The respect for the privacy of bodily functions corresponds to the respect for the distinction between social and private occasions; the back of the house is appropriately allocated to cooking, washing and excretory functions; the front parlour, distinguished from the living room-kitchen, is functionless except for public, social representation. Space by no means wasted, it is the face of the house, which speaks composedly and smiles for the rest of the body; from this room a person must rush if he bursts into tears. Certain families of the middle class tend to break down the barrier between public and private. They seek to live in public together in an unstructured, open room, expressing aptly (perhaps disastrously) their unstructured, personal system of control. In such a family it must be difficult to assimilate the image of society and the house to the image of body, and correspondingly more difficult, one suspects, for the individual to incorporate into his personal identity any symbolic structures integrating him with his own society. Hence it is predictable that the body may come to represent an alien husk, something from which the inmost self needs to escape, something whose exigencies should not be taken too seriously. It can and even must be transcended if the individual encased within the body is to fulfil his unique potential for experience. How brilliantly Bernstein's insight illuminates much of our contemporary culture. Alienation and integration imply different uses of the body as a symbolic mode. Is it legitimate to call them different codes derived from different social systems?

What has gone before has been stimulated by his work, yet I cannot pretend that I have so far succeeded in applying Bernstein's analysis of speech codes to other symbolic systems. It is not easy to distinguish the range from relatively restricted to elaborated ritual forms, which he suggests should be present in any medium as it is in speech. One might start by considering the possibility of the symbolic life being detached more and more from the task of relating an individual to his society and more and more freed for expressing his unique private concerns. This recalls again Lowie's use of Crow Indian beliefs to discredit Durkheim's theory of religion as always and essentially a collective experience. What type of primitive social structure would allow the symbolic orders to be relieved of their Durkheimian office of sustaining it? The question put in this form suggests that we should compare systems making progressively less and less claim on their individual members to honour a common morality. The weaker the social pressures, the freer the individual person. But this range of comparisons would merely show the diminishing moral and control aspects of the restricted code in some social systems. We still have to look for something corresponding to the division of labour among ourselves, some power to call forth an increasingly greater elaboration of the medium of expression towards greater universality in scope and greater syntactic flexibility. This power would create the need to communicate without the intimate knowledge of assumptions held in common. An interesting example would be the so-called 'mother-in-law language' of the Tully River aborigines. Robert Dixon says that the language of respect which a man uses for conversing with his mother-in-law expresses social distance by avoiding terms with particular reference and choosing generic terms.

Thus in the everyday language there are about a dozen terms for referring to types of grubs ... there is no generic term for 'grub' in the everyday language. However, in mother-in-law there is only a generic term ... (Dixon, 1968: 653)

This is a linguistic example. It would be a daunting task to analyse non-verbal rituals to see if any distinction between more particular and more universalistic symbols is ever organized to express two distinct ritual codes or even a gradation from one to another. However something suggestive of the elaborated code appears in the aesthetic activity of some New Guinea societies where art, like everything else, is harnessed to individual competition. Here is a challenge for students of primitive art to work out. Admittedly well beyond my own powers of scholarship, this suggestion does not exhaust the interest of pursuing the analogy of the restricted and elaborated code in ritual. However, my own interest is more concerned with varieties of restricted code.

Bernstein has allowed that there will be many different kinds of restricted codes. My classification of cosmologies is based on four social types: first, strong grid and group, the bounded system high on the classification line; second, a bounded, otherwise unstructured system (small group); and third, strong grid, in which the leaders are distinguished; and fourth, their mass of followers. If we ignore for the moment the latter two we can take together the two systems in which boundary is strong. Is it possible to see in the symbolism of the body appropriate to them two different restricted codes? In the one case, the religious emphasis would be expected to treat the body as the focus and symbol of life. We would expect to find positive themes of symbolic nourishment developed to the extent that the social body and the physical body are assimilated and both focus the identity of individuals in a structured, bounded system. In the second case, boundary without structure, that is, group without grid, we would expect to find the body an object of anxiety; fear of poisoning and debilitation would be dominant and ritual officiants much concerned with therapy, physical and social. Here, I suggest, we have two versions of a restricted code which serve the function of mediating the individual and his society by manipulating the image of the human body. Each type exerts its own constraints on the perceptions and thus on the choices of individuals; each symbolic system has its own pre-coded stimuli and responses which intimately affect the person's knowledge of his body and acts selectively on his capacity to respond to bodily images. They are restricted codes which integrate the individual with the social system.

In either of these two social types it is possible for sub-systems of a lower order of inclusiveness to be alienated from the whole. Then we can see another restricted code taking over. The body is still the image of society but somewhere inside it someone is not accepting its rule. I am suggesting that the symbolic medium of the body has its restricted code to express and sustain alienation of a sub-category from the wider society. In this code the claims of the body and of the wider society are not highly credited: bodily grooming, diet, pathology, these subjects attract less interest than other non-bodily claims. The body is despised and disregarded, consciousness is conceptually separated from its vehicle and accorded independent honour. Experimenting with consciousness becomes the most personal form of experience, contributing least to the widest social system, and therefore most approved. This is where the dichotomy of spirit and matter becomes an insistent theme.

If we allow that there is a restricted code for alienation, the way is open for a bold synthesis between the Durkheimian analysis of religious belief and theological controversies, whether from Christian, Islamic, Buddhist or Hindoo history. Edmund Leach has attempted to relate dogmas of virgin birth, a centrally Christian theme, to theories about the kind of dealings held in different cultures to be possible between gods and men (1966). He suggests that the problem is too complex for he, himself, to be satisfied with the correlations he draws. Indeed his attempt to make a plain sociological approach is less interesting than his attempts to find the local cultural patterns into which ideas about natural and divine procreation would seem to fit. The greatest value of this essay was his insistence that philosophical ideas about physical and metaphysical forces in the universe lie behind dogmas about whether humans and gods can mingle their natures or not. But where, we should ask, is any given balance between physical and other forces generated? Durkheim's famous saying

'Society is God', spelt out, means that in every culture where there is an image of society it is endowed with sacredness, or conversely that the idea of God can only be constituted from the idea of society. It follows from the first that alienation from society will be expressed by desacralizing its image. And from the second that the idea of God, dethroned from the centres of power, will be set up again in the small, interpersonal group which is alienated. Thus the image of God loses its majesty and becomes intimate, a personal friend who speaks directly, heart to heart without any truck with instituted forms. This is obvious and the change in the use of the body as a medium for expressing the sacred, from honouring the outside, shifts to honouring the interior exclusively. I shall now suggest that philosophical controversies about the relation of spirit to matter or mind to body be interpreted as exchanges of condensed statements about the relation of society to the individual.

Such controversies flare up and down. There may be no particular reason why they become active at one point in time and not in another. But I suggest that they only become relevant as metaphors when the relation of an alienated sub-group to the social whole becomes an acute political issue. The body or the flesh in these theological controversies represents the wider society; mind and spirit represent the individual identified with the sub-group concerned. To require a discussion to be conducted in those terms is like adopting a restricted speech code which is well understood by all parties. It governs the selections of symbolic relations and skews the judgements towards its own inherent values. To insist on the superiority of spiritual over material elements is to insist on the liberties of the individual and to imply a political programme to free him from unwelcome constraints.

In the contrary view, to declare that spirit works through matter, that spiritual values are made effective through material acts, that body and mind are intimately united, any emphasis on the necessity to mingle spirit and matter implies that the individual is by nature subordinate to society and finds his freedom within its forms. This view is prepared to sacralize flesh, while their opponents count it as blasphemy to teach the physical union of godhead and manhood.

The anthropologist can never assume that the chosen symbols of religious controversy are arbitrary. If they are used to discriminate contended positions, they also express something about the social situation. So it is that anthropologists cannot but admire the aptness of doctrines which deny that God could take human flesh for expressing a revolt against the established ecclesiastical order. In the early centuries of Christianity, when its doctrines were being refined and articulated, most of the theological disputes concerned the nature of the Second Person of the Trinity. As it finally emerged, the orthodox doctrine of the Incarnation insisted on a perfect mediation between spirit and matter. According to this creed, as defined at Nicea, Christ was fully God, fully man, both natures combined mysteriously in one person. The heresies of the third and fourth centuries which taught that Christ was mere man, not really God, or not fully man, an historical emanation from God, all agreed on admitting a gulf between spirit and matter. To move either way from the central doctrine of the Incarnation was to dilute the unique Christian message. Not so obviously, to move either way is to exalt spirit and debase matter and so to adopt the philosophical attitude which, following Durkheim's thought, is appropriate to detachment from or revolt against the established social forms. In his study of Arianism, John Henry Newman tended very much to treat the heresy itself as no more than a technique of revolt. For him it did not matter what bone of contention they chose, the contumacious behaviour of the heresiarchs was enough to show that their doctrine was of secondary interest (1901). It is certainly very difficult to demonstrate my thesis convincingly to historians because in the long time span of the institutions they study, a movement can start, like Arianism, as a discourse set in the restricted code of alienation, and quickly become one in the restricted code of integration, as when Constantius became Emperor and proclaimed Arianism as the official doctrine of Rome with himself as God's representative on earth. With Arian bishops installed in the great sees, the doctrines they espoused came to sound only hairsplittingly different from those they had so hotly rejected when the fight had been on, and general interest in the issues originally at stake dwindled to the basic symbols of allegiance to one side or another.

It is also difficult to demonstrate this theme in the field of Indian religion, because of its great complexity. What is claimed to be its special feature, the use of bodily purity to symbolize hierarchy and group boundaries, is in itself indeed only the natural system of symbols. India may well have developed the bodily mode to an unparalleled extent. If so, our approach would look, to explain its unique development, to the distinction between hierarchy and power, which Professor Dumont insists is a fundamental principle of the caste system (Dumont, 1966: 91–3). Where hierarchy is truly divorced from power, India would communicate within a restricted code of alienation. We would expect it to separate spirit from matter and to clothe the top ranks of the hierarchy in the most ethereal, non-physical symbols compatible with material comfort. Hence the austerities of the sects, which renounce the world by monastic withdrawal, would naturally provide the symbols of status for worldly and unworldly Brahmans, whose rank is defined by their opposition to the ruling caste. Setting a fashion in vegetarianism, both for gods and men, would appropriately be part of the move away from external, physically mediated religious forms towards the religion of the interior heart which is always preferred by preachers who themselves have withdrawn from temporal responsibility. Each sub-caste which tries to use this code for communicating with others about its relative status fails to realize the internal, spiritual changes which it implies. Each sub-caste is perforce involved in its local and political concerns. Consequently the speech of renunciation from the material world takes on a spectacularly material meaning: formal spirituality becomes hidebound in material gestures and serves very earthy, political ends. The Indian sub-continent, in so far as its use of the bodily medium is peculiar, surely owes this development to the strong disestablishmentarianism of its official church, implicit in the doctrine of hierarchy divorced from power. Conversely, the

Church of Rome would owe its own parallel and distinctive development of doctrine to its early association of religious hierarchy with power. In saying this I do not wish to allot the primacy in determining ritual forms to ideological bias. As I see it, essentially it is initially in small decisions, about who deals with whom and how, that these codes develop. As the doctrines and social forms interact, they develop momentum and finally come to create a symbolic environment in which later generations of individuals find themselves. But, however strong the power of this symbolic medium to coerce subsequent choices, just because it is a system, it can be cracked whenever any part of it is breached: thus the original Protestantism; thus the changes in the caste system.

Jung reproached Protestant Europe for giving up its austerity and seeking to parade in the finery of Eastern religions. In a passage which reveals his own abdication of judgement to a restricted code of alienation, he applauds the loss of meaning of the old religious symbols of Christianity, as a noble stripping of outer meaningless husks down to the bare individual self. Having achieved so much, what a falling off he sees in the embracing of alien religious forms:

> If he should now go and cover his nakedness with the gorgeous dress of the Orient, like the theosophists, he would be untrue to his own history. A man does not work his way down to beggarhood and then pose as an Indian king on the stage. (Jung, 1940: 63)

But there was no switch in logic and no betrayal of the principles of Protestantism in the theosophist turning to exotic cultures, only a natural evolution. For a European turning to Eastern doctrines is a European rejecting the Christian gospel of God taking flesh. First the Eucharist, then inevitably sooner or later the Incarnation; for the same social process which made the first repugnant was bound to lead to the rejection of the other. To the extent that society contains individuals united to it by no strong, solidary bonds, their culture is likely to believe romantically in the separation of pure spirit from gross matter, to seek to embrace the one and somehow at the same time to reject the other.

It may be that in this century we have become more aware of the subjective conditions of experience. Certainly it seems that the possibilities of self-awareness are here. But the practical problem of retaining consciousness is as great as ever. Lévi-Strauss has sought to display the action of the unconscious mind expressing itself through social forms. He argues that a moiety system, in which society divides itself into two wife-exchanging halves, makes a visible representation of the mind's natural proclivity to divide and subdivide (1968a: 132f.). The worldwide distribution of moiety systems, their appearance in the most simple and small-scale societies, their persistence, all suggest that by studying moieties we can do a kind of social archaeology. Understanding how a moiety system has power over its members is like digging into the prehistory of mankind in an area which picks and shovels never reach. By binary distinctions our cave-ancestors may have created the contrast of culture/nature, started all the contrasts on which language is built, and even created their society in the image of mind. This is Lévi-Strauss's implied argument.

Mercifully, we are not in thrall at present to that particular surge of creativity which produces dualist organization. Our society is not restricted to the moiety system. But unless reflection on the self-sustaining power of moieties warns us of the power of our own unconscious mental activity, these lessons of prehistory are surely wasted. The resilience of primitive moiety systems shows how difficult it is to break out of the circle, once it is set up, between the impulse of unconscious mind and its external expression. How many people have smiled knowingly at the scribblings on the walls of the Latin Quarter during the 1968 revolts in Paris. 'La honte est contre-Révolutionnaire' and 'Le discours est contre-Révolutionnaire'. But intellectuals are slow to see their own behaviour in the same light as that of the rioters tearing up paving stones. 'Plus je fais la Révolution, plus j'ai envie de faire l'amour'. Reforming bishops and radical theologians, to say nothing of Utopian marxists, must eventually recognize that the generous warmth of their doctrinal latitude, their critical dissolving of categories and attack on intellectual and administrative distinctions are generated by analogous social experience. 'Ears have walls'. Another of the graffiti of Paris 1968 refers summarily to vain supplications and hardened rejection. No judgement is intended here on the political accuracy of that slogan at that place and time. As a general statement for the sociology of perception it could be amended to 'Ears must have walls'. Legitimacy must be clothed in magic, words must be made into things, blocks, hedges, compartments are the condition of knowledge. Thinkers must recognize the destructive lure of the natural system of symbols, equally when it devastates category boundaries as when it wrongfully closes them.

Returning to our opening theme, we find that the apparent anti-ritualism of today is the adoption of one set of natural symbols in place of another. It is like a switch between restricted speech codes. Two morals can be drawn from this analogy; first the duty of everyone to preserve their vision from the constraints of the natural symbols when judging any social situation; second the opportunity of religious bodies to set their message in the natural system of symbols. For the first duty, we must recognize that the value of particular social forms can only be judged objectively by the analytic power of the elaborated code. Beware, therefore, of arguments couched in the bodily medium. Strongly subjective attitudes to society get coded through bodily symbols.

For the second, Christian preachers fail to respond to the current meaning in the body. The elaborated code has here intervened too much. Or perhaps the difference of age separating those in authority from those in immediate contact with the faithful may explain the neglect in religion of symbols which are being spontaneously exploited elsewhere. The very religious themes which repelled radicals of half a century ago are now being seized upon in drama, fiction and visual art and woven into a secular symbolic system. We may well ask why the now elderly radicals rejected religious themes of renunciation, why they disdained the unabashed, sexual imagery of the mystics and the completely counter-rational doctrine of the resurrection of the body, and why the young radicals of today express contempt for the physical body, read the mystics and cultivate non-rationality.

The difference surely lies in the respective attitudes to political power, the former seeking and the latter rejecting it. The Churches could worry that their clothes are being stolen while they bathe in a stream of ethical sensitivity. For the current dichotomy of spirit and matter is an assertion of spiritual values. While preaching good works they would do well to relate the simple social duty to the wealth of doctrines which in Christian history have done service for the same restricted code: the mystical body, the communion of saints, death, resurrection, immortality and speaking with tongues.

Bibliography

ABERLE, DAVID: *The Peyote Religion among the Navaho*, London, Aldine, 1966.

AUERBACH, ERICH: *Literary Language and Its Public*, London, Routledge & Kegan Paul ,1965.

BARTH, FREDRIK: *Nomads of South Persia. The Basseri Tribe of the Khamseh Confederacy*, London, Allen & Unwin, 1964.

BARTHES, ROLAND: *Writing Degree Zero*, London, Jonathan Cape, 1967.

BARTON, R. F.: *Ifugao Law:* University of California Publications in American Archaeology and Ethnology, 15. 1: 186ff., 1919.

Ifugao Economics: University of California Publications in American Archaeology and Ethnology, 15. 5: 385–446, 1922.

The Religion of the Ifugaos, Memoirs of American Anthropological Association, No. 65, 1946.

The Kalingas: Their Institutions and Custom Law, University of Chicago Publications in Anthropology, Social Anthropology Series, Chicago, University of Chicago Press, 1949.

BERGER, P. and LUCKMANN, T.: *The Social Construction of Reality, and Treatise in the Sociology of Knowledge*, New York, Doubleday, 1966.

BERNSTEIN, BASIL: 'Some Sociological Determinants of Perception', *British Journal of Sociology*, 9: 159; 174, 1958.

'A Public Language – Some Sociological Implications of a Linguistic Form', *British Journal of Sociology*, 10: 311–26, 1959.

'Linguistic Codes, Hesitation Phenomena and Intelligence', *Language and Speech*, 5. 1. October–December: 31–46, 1962.

'Social Class and Psycho-therapy', *British Journal of Sociology*, 15: 54–64, 1964.

'A Socio-Linguistic Approach to Social Learning', *Penguin Survey of the Social Sciences*, Gould, J. (ed.) ,London, Penguin, 1965.

'A Socio-Linguistic Approach to Socialisation' in Gumperz, J. and D. Hymes (ed.), *Directions in Socio-Linguistics*, New York, Holt, Rinehart & Winston, 1970.

Class, Codes and Control, Vol. I, *Theoretical Studies towards a Sociology of Language*, London, Routledge & Kegan Paul, 1971.

BERNSTEIN, B., H. L. ELVIN, and R. S. PETERS: *Ritual in Education*, Philosophical Transactions of the Royal Society, Series B, Biological Sciences, No. 772, Vol. 251: 429–36, 1966.

BRADDON, R.: *Roy Thomson of Fleet Street*, London, Collins, 1965.

BROWN, PETER: *Augustine of Hippo*, London, Faber & Faber, 1967.

BULMER, RALPH: 'Why is the Cassowary not a Bird?' *Man*, N. S. 2, 1: 5–25, 1967.

BURRIDGE, KENELM: *Mambu, a Melanesian Millennium*, London, Methuen, 1960.

'Tangu, Northern Madang District' in Lawrence, P. and M. J. Meggitt (ed.), *Gods, Ghosts and Men in Melanesia*, London, Oxford University Press, 1965.

BUXTON, JEAN: 'The Mandari of the Southern Sudan' in Middleton, J. and D. Tait (ed.), *Tribes without Rulers*, London, Routledge & Kegan Paul, 1958.

Chiefs and Strangers, Oxford, Clarendon, 1963.

'Mandari Witchcraft' in Middleton, J. and E. Winter (ed.), *Witchcraft and Sorcery in East Africa*, London, Routledge & Kegan Paul, 1963.

'Animals, Identity and Human Peril. Some Mandari Images', *Man*, N. S. 3. 1: 35–49, 1968.

CALLEY, MALCOLM J. C.: *God's People: West Indian Pentecostal Sects in England*, London, Oxford University Press for Institute of Race Relations, 1965.

CLARK, FRANCIS: *The Eucharistic Sacrifice and the Reformation*, London, The Newman Press, 1960.

COAD, F. ROY: *A History of the Brethren Movement*, London, Paternoster Press, 1968.

COHN, NORMAN: *The Pursuit of the Millennium*, London, Secker & Warburg, 1957.

'Mediaeval Millenarism: Its Bearings on the Comparative Study of Millenarian Movements' in Thrupp, Sylvia (ed.), *Millennial Dreams in Action*, The Hague, Mouton, 1962.

COX, HARVEY: *The Secular City*, London, Penguin, 1968.

DE COPPET, DANIEL: 'Pour une étude des échanges cérémoniels en Mélanésie', *L'Homme*, 8. 4: 45–57, 1968.

Bibliography

DIXON, R.: 'Correspondence: Virgin Birth', *Man*, N. S. 3. 4: 653–4, 1968.

DOUGLAS, MARY: *The Lele of the Kasai*, London, Oxford University Press, 1963.

Purity and Danger: An Analysis of Concepts of Pollution and Taboo, London, Routledge & Kegan Paul, 1966.

Pollution in *International Encyclopedia of the Social Sciences*, Vol. 12: 336–42, New York, Macmillan and the Free Press, 1968a.

'The Relevance of Tribal Studies', *Journal of Psychosomatic Research*, 12. 1, 1968b.

'Social Control of Cognition. Factors in Joke Perception', *Man*, N. S. 3. 3: 361–67, 1968c.

DUCHESNE-GUILLEMIN, L.: *The Western Response to Zoroaster: Ratanbei Katrak Lectures*, 1956, Oxford, Clarendon, 1958.

DUMONT, LOUIS: *Homo Hierarchicus – essai sur le système des castes*, Paris, Gallimard, 1966.

DURKHEIM, ÉMILE: *Element~ ~ns of the Religious Life* (translated by J. W. S~ain) ~ ~on, Allen & Unwin, 1915.

DURKHEIM, E., and MAUSS, M.: *Primitive Classification*, 1903, translated with an introduction by Rodney Needham, London, Cohen & West, 1963.

EPISTEMON: *Ces idées qui ont ébranlé la France*, Nanterre, Fayard, 1968.

EVANS-PRITCHARD, E. E.: *The Nuer, a Description of the Modes of Livelihood and Political Institutions of a Nilotic People*, Oxford, Clarendon, 1940a.

'The Nuer of the Southern Sudan' in Fortes, M. and E. E. Evans-Pritchard (ed.), *African Political Systems*, London, Oxford University Press, 1940b.

Nuer Religion, Clarendon, Oxford, 1956.

FANON, F.: *The Wretched of the Earth*, London, MacGibbon & Kee, 1965.

FIRTH, R.: *Tikopia Ritual and Belief*, London, Allen & Unwin, 1967.

FORTES, MEYER: *The Dynamics of Clanship among the Tallensi*, London, Oxford University Press for the International African Institute, 1945.

The Web of Kinship among the Tallensi, London, Oxford University Press for the International African Institute, 1949.

Oedipus and Job in West African Religion, Cambridge University Press, 1959.

Totem and Taboo, Presidential address 1966, *Proceedings of the Royal Anthropological Institute*, 1967.

FORTUNE, R. F.: *The Sorcerers of Dobu*, London, 1932.

FREEDMAN, M.: *Presidential Address to the Royal Anthropological Institute*, Proceedings, 1969.

GOFFMAN, E.: *The Presentation of the Self in Everyday Life*, Edinburgh, University of Edinburgh Social Research Centre, 1956.

GOODENOUGH, E. R.: *Jewish Symbols in the Graeco-Roman Period*, Vol. 5, New York, Bollingen Foundation, 1956; London, Oxford University Press, 1968.

GRÖNBECH, W.: *The Culture of the Teutons*, Vol. 1, London, Oxford University Press, 1931.

GULLIVER, P. H.: *Neighbours and Networks: The Idiom of Kinship in Social Action among the Ndendeuli of Tanzania*, California, University of California Press, 1971.

HALL, EDWARD T.: *The Silent Language*, New York, Doubleday, 1959.

HARRINGTON, MICHAEL: *The Other America*, New York, Macmillan, 1962; London, Penguin, 1968.

HERBERG, WILL: *Protestant, Catholic, Jew*, London, Mayflower, 1960.

HIGHER CATECHETICAL INSTITUTE: Nijmegen: *A New Catechism, Catholic Faith for Adults*, London, Burns & Oates, 1967.

HORTON, ROBIN: *Book review:* 'Divinity and Experience', *Africa*, 32. 1: 78, 1962.

'Types of Spirit Possession in Kalabari Religion', in *Spirit Mediumship and Society in Africa*, John Beattie and John Middleton, (ed.), London, Routledge & Kegan Paul, 1969.

HUMPHRY, C. E.: *Manners for Women*, London, James Bowden, 1897.

JACOBS, PAUL and SAUL LANDAU: *The New Radicals, a Report with Documents*, London, Penguin, 1967.

JUNG, CARL G.: *The Integration of the Personality*, London, Routledge & Kegan Paul, 1940.

KEYNES, J. M.: *Essays in Biography* (*Mr Lloyd George*), London, Macmillan, 1933.

KLEIN, MELANIE: *Envy and Gratitude, a Study of Unconscious Sources*, London, Tavistock, 1957.

Our Adult World and Other Essays, London, Heinemann, 1963.

KLUCKHOHN, CLYDE: *Navaho Witchcraft*, Cambridge, Mass., Peabody Museum, 1944.

KNIGHTLEY, PHILLIP, and COLIN SIMPSON, *The Secret Lives of Lawrence of Arabia*, London, Nelson, 1969.

LAWRENCE, P.: *Road Belong Cargo: a Study of the Cargo Movement in the Southern Madang District, New Guinea*, Manchester, Manchester University Press, 1964.

Bibliography

LAWRENCE, P. and M. J. MEGGITT (ed.): *Gods, Ghosts and Men in Melanesia: Some Religions of Australia, New Guinea and the New Hebrides*, London, Oxford University Press, 1965.

LEACH, E. R.: *Virgin Birth*, Henry Myers Lecture, Proceedings of the Royal Anthropological Institute: 33–39, 1966.

LÉVI-STRAUSS, C.: Introduction to Marcel Mauss, *Sociologie et anthropologie*, Paris, Presses Universitaires de France, 1950.

Mythologiques I: Le cru et le cuit, Paris, Plon, 1964.

Mythologiques II: Du miel aux cendres, Paris, Plon, 1966.

Mythologiques III: L'Origine des manières de table, Paris, Plon, 1968a.

Structural Anthropology, London, Allen Lane, Penguin Press, 1968b.

LEWIS, I. M.: 'Spirit Possession and Deprivation Cults', *Man*, N. S. 1, 3: 307–29, 1966.

LIENHARDT, GODFREY: 'Some Notions of Witchcraft among the Dinka', *Africa*, 21. 1: 303–18, 1951.

'The Western Dinka' in Middleton, J. and D. Tait (ed.), *Tribes without Rulers*, London, Routledge & Kegan Paul, 1958.

Divinity and Experience: The Religion of the Dinka, Oxford, Clarendon, 1961.

'The Situation of Death: An Aspect of Anuak Philosophy', *Anthropological Quarterly*, 35. 2. April: 74–85, 1962.

LOWIE, R. H.: *Primitive Religion*, London, Routledge & Kegan Paul, 1925.

MAIMONIDES, MOSES: *The Guide for the Perplexed*, translated from the Arabic by M. Friedlander, London, Routledge & Kegan Paul, 1956.

MARSHALL, LORNA: '!Kung Bushman Religious Beliefs', *Africa*, 32. 3: 221–52, 1962.

MARTIN, DAVID: 'Towards Eliminating the Concept of Secularisation', *Penguin Survey of the Social Sciences*, Gould, J. (ed.)., London, Penguin, 1965.

MARWICK, M. G.: 'Another Modern Anti-Witchcraft Movement in East Central Africa', *Africa*, 20. 2: 100–12, 1950.

'The Social Context of Cewa Witch Beliefs', *Africa*, 22. 2: 120–35; 215–33, 1952.

Sorcery in its Social Setting, a Study of the Northern Rhodesia Cewa, Manchester, Manchester University Press, 1965.

MAUSS, MARCEL: 'Les Techniques du corps', *Journal de la Psychologie*, 32. March–April, 1936.

MEGGITT, M. J. 'The Mae Enga of the Western Highlands' in Lawrence,

P. and M. J. Meggitt (ed.), *Gods, Ghosts and Men in Melanesia*, London, Oxford University Press, 1965.

MERTON, R. K.: *Social Theory and Social Structure* (revised edn), Glencoe, The Free Press, 1957.

MIDDLETON, J. and DAVID TAIT (ed.): *Tribes without Rulers. Studies in African Segmentary Systems*, London, Routledge & Kegan Paul, 1958.

MIDDLETON, JOHN: *The Religion of the Lugbara*, International African Institute, London, Oxford University Press, 1960.

MITCHELL, CLYDE: *The Yao Village*, Manchester, Manchester University Press, 1956.

NEAL, SISTER MARIE AUGUSTA: *Values and Interests in Social Change*, London, Prentice-Hall, 1965.

NEEDHAM, RODNEY: 'Percussion and Transition', *Man*, N. S. 2. 4: 606–14, 1967.

NEWFIELD, JACK: *A Prophetic Minority: The American New Left*, London, Anthony Blond, 1966.

NEWMAN, J. H.: *The Arians of the Fourth Century*, London, Longman, 1901.

OLIVER, D. L.: *Human Relations and Language in a Papuan-Speaking Tribe of Southern Bougainville, Solomon Islands*. Papers of the Peabody Museum, Vol. 29. 2: 3–38, 1949.

A Solomon Island Society: Kinship and Leadership among the Siuai of Bougainville, London, Oxford University Press, 1957.

OTTO, RUDOLPH: *The Idea of the Holy*, London, Oxford University Press, 1957.

PARSONS, T. and NEIL SMELSER: *Society and Economy*, London, Routledge & Kegan Paul, 1956.

PAUL VI: *Encyclical letter: Mysterium Fidei*, 1965.

Decree: Paenitemine, 1966.

RICHARDS, A. I.: 'A Modern Movement of Witch-Finders', *Africa*, 8. 4: 448–61, 1935.

RIVIÈRE, PETER: 'Factions and Exclusions in Two South American Village Systems', *Witchcraft Confessions and Accusations*, ed. Mary Douglas, A.S.A. Monograph No. 9, London, Tavistock, 1970.

ROVERE, RICHARD: *Senator Joe McCarthy*, New York, Harcourt, Brace & World, 1959.

SACRED CONGREGATION OF RITES: *Instruction on the Worship of the Eucharistic Mystery*, London, Catholic Truth Society, 1967.

SARTRE, JEAN-PAUL: *Words*, London, Hamish Hamilton, 1964.

Bibliography

SMELSER, NEIL J.: *Theory of Collective Behaviour*, London, Routledge & Kegan Paul, 1962.

SMITH, W. R.: *Lectures on the Religion of the Semites*, London, Black, 1894.

SPENCER, PAUL: *The Samburu: A Study of Gerontocracy in a Nomadic Tribe*, London, Routledge & Kegan Paul, 1965.

STRINDBERG, AUGUST: *The Son of a Servant: The Story of the Evolution of a Human Being 1849–67*, London, Jonathan Cape, 1967.

STRIZOWER, S.: 'Clean and Unclean', *Jewish Chronicle* (London), 26 August 1966.

TAYLOR, A. J. P.: *English History 1914–1945*, Oxford, Clarendon, 1965.

THRUPP, SYLVIA L. (ed.): *Millennial Dreams in Action. Essays in Comparative Study*, The Hague, Mouton, 1962.

TREVOR-ROPER, H. R.: *Religion, the Reformation and Social Change and Other Essays*, London, Macmillan, 1967.

TURNBULL, COLIN M.: *The Forest People*, London, Chatto & Windus, 1961.

Wayward Servants: The Two Worlds of the African Pygmies, London, Eyre & Spottiswoode, 1965.

TURNER, V. W.: *Chihamba, the White Spirit. A Ritual Drama of the Ndembu*, Manchester, Manchester University Press, 1962.

The Drums of Affliction: A Study of Religious Processes among the Ndembu of Zambia, International Africa Institute, Oxford, Clarendon, 1968.

VAN GENNEP, A.: *The Rites of Passage* (translated by M. B. Vizedom and G. L. Caffee), London, Routledge & Kegan Paul, 1960.

WEIL, SIMONE: *Waiting on God*, London, Routledge & Kegan Paul, 1951.

WILSON, BRYAN R. (ed.): *Patterns of Sectarianism*, London, Heinemann Educational Books, 1967.

WOODBURN, JAMES: *The Social Organization of the Hadza of North Tanganyika*, Doctoral thesis, University of Cambridge, 1964.

WORSLEY, PETER: *The Trumpet Shall Sound: a Study of 'Cargo' Cults in Melanesia*, London, MacGibbon & Kee, 1957.

Index

Index

Index

214

Mary Douglas was educated at a Sacred Heart
Convent in London (hence her permanent
interest in the sociology of religion) and at Oxford
where she studied Philosophy, Politics, and
Economics. Her first job was in the Colonial
Office (1943–6), where she developed an interest
in Africa and was able to meet anthropologists
engaged in war work in the Civil Service. She
returned to Oxford in 1947 to take a B.Sc. in
anthropology. From 1949–50, and again in
1953, she did fieldwork in the Belgian Congo.
Since 1951 she has been a member of the
Anthropology Department at University College
London and in 1970 she became Professor of
Social Anthropology there. Her publications
include *The Lele of the Kasai* and *Purity and
Danger*. She married James Douglas in 1951,
and they have three children.